Mohamed Minkailou

Attitudes towards the Use of Songhay as a Language of Education in Gao (Mali)

Mohamed Minkailou

Attitudes towards the Use of Songhay as a Language of Education in Gao (Mali)

LAP LAMBERT Academic Publishing

Publisher:
LAP LAMBERT Academic Publishing
is a trademark of
Dodo Books Indian Ocean Ltd., member of the OmniScriptum S.R.L Publishing group
str. A.Russo 15, of. 61, Chisinau-2068, Republic of Moldova Europe
Printed at: see last page
ISBN: 978-620-2-52725-5

Summary

The choice of a language of education and people's support of that language, have always been a great concern for most Sub-Saharan African countries. Mali is no exception. At independence, and for the preservation of national unity, the Malian government opted for the colonial French language as its sole language of education, administration, politics, etc. The limitations to that language policy later on drove successive governments to gradually introduce the native languages into the educational system. However, after the experimentation, introduction, and generalisation of those languages into the educational system, very few (if any) studies have been carried out to determine the attitudes and behaviours of the people whose children use them as media of education at school.

This research was conducted to determine how people of Gao feel about and behave towards Songhay as the language of education of their children at school. In other words, the issue under investigation is the determination of the attitudes and behaviours of people towards two pedagogical innovations, *Convergent Pedagogy* and the *Curriculum* that make use of Songhay as a medium of instruction at school.

To determine the attitudes and behaviours, the researcher carried out a survey in the Commune of Gao. He administered two questionnaires, one to headmasters and another to teachers, both classical and bilingual. The questionnaires were coupled with interviews with Parent Teacher Associations, bilingual and classical school pupils, School Management Committees, Child Mother Associations, laymen, and Non-Governmental Organisation representatives working in the sector of education in the Commune.

The findings of the investigation revealed that the majority of people in the Commune of Gao are, not just reluctant, but reject the use of Songhay as a medium of education in their schools, and by the same token, advocate the former classical French-based system. Literate people and the wealthy ones in particular, would just withdraw their children from public bilingual schools and send them to private classical schools, even if they had to pay huge tuition fees.

The reasons behind such prevailing negative attitudes and behaviours among these people are various: lack of teacher training in bilingual education, lack of teaching material for both teachers and pupils, and lack of information and sensitisation about the use of Songhay in bilingual education.

The recommendations the researcher proposes include the training of all teachers (since bilingual education is in generalisation) in the use of the native languages in formal

i

education, the development and availability of teaching material, and the information and sensitisation of all citizens about the benefits of bilingual education.

Dedication

The present work is dedicated to:

-My late father and mother;

-My wife and my children.

Table of contents

List of tables

List of acronyms

ACALAN: Académie Africaine des Langues (African Language Academy).

ACAS: Non Governmental Organisation in the Commune of Gao.

ACCT: Agence de Coopération Culturelle et Technique (Cultural and Technical Cooperation Agency).

ARECDEV: Non Governmental Organisation in the Commune of Gao.

CAF : Centre d'Alphabétisation Fonctionnelle (Functional Literacy Centre).

CAP : Centre d'Animation Pédagogique (Pedagogical Animation Centre).

CED: Centre d'Education pour le Développment (Centre of Education for Development).

CEDRAB: Higher Islamic Studies Institute (in Timbuktu).

CEPE : Certificat d'Etudes Primaires Elémentaires (Basic Education Certificate).

CIAVER: Centre International Audio-Visuel d'Etudes et de Recherche (International Centre for Audio-Visual Studies and Research).

CMA : Child Mother Association.

CMDT: Companie Malienne de Développment des Textiles (Malian Company for the Development of Textile).

CNA : Centre National de l'Alphabétisation (National Literacy Centre).

CNAF : Centre National de l'Alphabétisation Fonctionnelle (National Centre for Functional Literacy).

CNE: Centre National de l'Education (National Education Centre).

CNR-ENF : Centre National des Ressources de l'Education Non-Formelle (National Centre of Non-Formal Education Resources).

CNRST: Centre National de Recherche Scientifique et Technologique (National Centre for Scientific and Technological Research).

CRADE: Non Governmental Organisation in the Commune of Gao.

CRES: Centre Régional de l'Energie Solaire (Regional Centre of Solar Energy)

DNAFLA : Directional Nationale de l'Alphabétisation Fonctionnnelle et de la Linguistique

DNEB : Direction Nationale de l'Education de Base (National Directorate of Basic Education).

DP ECM : Développement de la Personne-Education Civique et Morale.

DP EPS : Développement de la Personne- Education Physique et Sportive (

DRAFLA : Direction Régionale de l'Alphabétisation Fonctionnelle et de la Linguistique Appliquée (Regional Directorate for Functional Literacy and Applied Linguistics).

DRE : Direction Régionale de l'Education (Regional Education Directorate).

x

Appliquée (National Directorate for Functional Literacy and Applied Linguistics).

EFA : Education For All.

ENA: Ecole Nationale d'Administration (National School of Administration).

ENI: Ecole Nationale des Ingénieurs (National School of Ingineers).

ENSup: Ecole Normale Supérieure (Teacher Training College).

ESITEX: Ecole Secondaire d'Industrie et des Textiles (Industry and Textile Secondary School).

FAST: Faculté des Sciences et Techniques (School of Science and Techniques).

FLASH: Faculté des Lettres, Langues, Arts et Sciences Humaines (Humanities).

FMPOS: Faculté de Médecine, de Pharmacie et d'OdontoStomatologie (

FNUAP : Fonds des Nations Unies pour la Population (United Nations' Population Fund).

FSJE: Faculté des Sciences Juridiques et Economiques (School of Law and Economics).

GAIRD: Non Governmental Organisation in the Commune of Gao.

GRAIP: Non Governmental Organisation in the Commune of Gao.

GREFFA: Non Governmental Organisation in the Commune of Gao.

IFM : Institut de Formation des Maîtres (Teacher Training Institute).

IGM: Institut Géographique du Mali (Malian Geographical Institute).

ILAB: Institut des Langues Abdoulaye Barry (Abdoulaye Barry Language Institute).

INAFLA: Institut National pour l'Alphabétisation Fonctionnelle et de la Linguistique Appliquée (National Institute for Functional Literacy and Applied Linguistics).

IPN: Institut Pedagogique National (National Pedagogical Institute)

IPR-IFRA: Institut Polytechnique Rurale -Institut de Formation et de Recherche Appliquée (

ISFRA: Institut Supérieur de Formation et de Recherche Appliquée (Higher Institute for Training and Applied Research).

IUG: Institut Universitaire de Gestion (University Institute of Management).

LC: Langue et Communication (Language and Communication).

MACALAN: Mission de l'Académie Africaine des Langues (African Language Academy Mission).

MEN : Ministère de l'Education Nationale (Ministry of National Education).

MT : Mathématiques and Technologie (Mathematic and Technology).

NEF : Nouvelle Ecole Fondamentale (New Basic Education).

NGO: Non-Governmental Organisation.

N R: National Road.

NTIC : Nouvelles Technologies de l'Information et de la Communication (New Technologies of Information and Communication).

OAU: Organisation of African Unity.

OXFAM GB: Non Governmental Organisation in the Commune of Gao.

PEMA : Programme Expérimental Mondial de l'Alphabétisation (World Experimental Literacy Programme).

PC: Pédagogie Convergente (Convergent Pedagogy).

PRODEC: Programme de Développement de l'Education (Education Development Programme).

PTA : Parent Teacher Association.

RACE : Recensement Administratif à Caractère Electoral (Electoral Administrative Census).

SEAD: Non Governmental Organisation in Gao.

SH: Sciences Humaines (Humanities).

SIL : Société Internationale de Linguistique (International Linguistic Society).

SMC : School Management Committee.

SMT: Sciences, Mathématiques et Technologie (Science, Mathematic and Technology).

SOTELMA : Société de Télécommunication du Mali (Malian Telecommunication Company).

ST: Sciences et Techniques (Science and Techniques).

SUCO: Non Governmental Organisation in the Commune of Gao.

TASSAGHT: Non Governmental Organisation in the Commune of Gao.

UNESCO: United Nations' Educational, Scientific and Cultural Organisation.

UNICEF: United Nations International Children's Emergency Fund.

USAID: United States' Agency for International Development.

Acknowledgements

I would like to express my deep gratitude to Mamadou GUEYE for his guidance, open-mindedness, encouragement and significant contribution. I am indebted to Youssouf HAIDARA at DNEB for his kindness, availability and help, especially at the initial stage of this research. He provided me with valuable information and material. My sincere thanks go to Marguerite CANVIN (SIL) for her advice, encouragement and assistance. She helped me a lot with various kinds of material. She also proofread my questionnaires before their administration. My sincere thanks also go to Rosemary TRAORÉ (a Fulbright Scholar at FLASH) for proofreading this work.

I would like to express my deep gratitude to the headmasters of Gadeye A and Farandjireye B schools, the teachers of the two schools, and their pupils. My special thanks are also addressed to Mr. Konipo, the headmaster of Farandjireye C School (now in retirement), who introduced me to the other headmasters.

Introduction

Language is a means of communication and interaction used by social groups to express their feelings, needs, desires, and aspirations and to share experience. A person may use different languages which do not always hold the same status both at the level of the user and the whole nation. That is why language specialists draw a distinction between a mother tongue, a second language, a foreign language, a national language and an official language. They all serve the purpose of communication, but in different contexts.

A mother tongue is a language usually acquired right from birth in the family circle. Its acquisition is natural and unconscious as no special teaching is required; mothers and caretakers do however undertake such teaching enterprise with the repetition of words, phrases, the use of expansions and reinforcement. The view behind such an enterprise is that the child will not succeed without assistance from caretakers. However, evidence from child language acquisition research shows that the only requirements for language acquisition are the exposure to the language and the possession of appropriate mental capacities.

A *first language* acquired becomes part of the user's identity, culture, and roots. Language is an aspect of the cultural heritage of the individual; consequently language acquisition or learning becomes part of cultural learning. So to be denied one's language is tantamount to being denied one's culture and identity (F. West, 1975).

A *second language* is any language learnt right after the mother tongue. It becomes official when it is recognised by the national assembly as the medium to be used by the administration, school, government, and politicians of the country. T. Skutnabb-Kangas (1981, p.141) defines it as a language:

Used daily in the speaker's own environment, perhaps not in the immediate environment, at least in early childhood, but at any rate in the larger community. As soon as one is outside one's own home, there will be a chance (or a risk of being forced) to use the language actively, or at any rate one will hear it used.

In some cases, a second language, usually inherited from colonisation, becomes a country's official language: many countries around the world were colonised by Europeans who imposed their languages. Even after independence, those languages have continued to be used in the administration and at school as media of instruction, etc; English in the former British colonies and French in the former French colonies play this role. They, at least, help maintain cohesion among ethnic groups that have different languages: in some African countries, there are more than three hundred languages.

1

There are however countries where the second language and the official language are quite distinct. In the Maghrebian countries, for instance, Arabic is both the national and the official language whereas French is used as a second language.

A *foreign language* is normally taught and learnt as a school subject. It plays little or no role in everyday communication in the area where it is learnt. T. Skutnabb-Kangas (1981, p.141) argues that *"learning a foreign language is learning a language not used [by the speaker or by others] in the immediate environment as a daily means of communication"*. An illustration is the learning and use of English in French-speaking Africa.

A lot of people around the world speak more than just a mother tongue. Globalisation appears to be conducive to the development of bilingualism (or multilingualism) and the use of bilingual education. In this sense, different types of *bilingualism* and *bilingual education* have been proposed (W. Grabe and R. B. Kaplan, 1992; T. Skutnabb-Kangas, 1981; D. Crystal, 2003). Definitions of bilingualism range from the ability to utter a meaningful phrase to native-like ability in the two languages (for instance, the four language skills). Research identifies three levels of bilingualism: individual, group, and national.

A distinction has been observed between two types of bilingualism: *additive bilingualism* in which case the mother tongue is being preserved while a second language is acquired, and *substractive bilingualism* in which case the mother tongue is not being developed and preserved, or is even being discouraged.

T. Skutnab-Kangas (1981, p.95) makes a distinction between three types of bilingualism. *Natural bilingualism* involves an individual who learns two languages without formal education, usually at a younger age over time. *School bilingualism*, on the other hand, involves a person learning a second or foreign language via formal teaching. Close to school bilingualism is *cultural bilingualism* which involves adults learning a foreign language for work or travel purposes.

A further distinction has been drawn between *elite bilingualism* (a highly educated person who has received part of his or her education in a foreign language with opportunities to use that language in a natural way) and *folk bilingualism* (people who have been obliged to learn the other language because they come from a linguistic minority or from third world oppressed linguistic majorities). In the same vein, an individual will be said to be *bilingual* (or *multilingual*) when his *"linguistic ability in two (or more) languages is similar to that of a native speaker"* (K. Malmkjaer, 2000, p.57). A *balanced* bilingual also called an *equilingual* (very rare) is a person who roughly has the same ability in the two languages.

2

A further distinction has also been drawn between a *primary* (natural) and a *secondary* bilingual. The former, close to T. Skuttnabb-Kangass' Natural Bilingual, has acquired the two languages in a natural way (i. e., the language of the family circle is different from that of the larger social group); the latter has learnt one of the languages through a formal process of instruction (i. e., one language was naturally acquired at home, the other at school). The second instance remains the commonest in colonised sub-Saharan Africa where the child's mother tongue and his language of school education are usually different. In this case, the child cannot avoid becoming bilingual if s/he wants to benefit from the educational system of the country.

There are varied views about the best strategy to introduce students to a language of education that is different from the home language or the one used in the wider social group. Two approaches have been proposed:

i) Mother-tongue teaching. In this case, *"children are first taught all their subjects in their mother tongue. The school language will be introduced gradually, and may then either take over completely, or both languages may continue to be used side by side"* (K. Malmkjaer, 2000, p.57)

D. Crystal (2002, p.368) holds a closer view when he defends that children *"should therefore be educated in their mother tongue only until they are able to continue in the majority language,"* and,

ii) Teaching in the school language exclusively with the introduction of the other (local) languages as school subjects only.

Advocates for bilingual education recognise the advantages and drawbacks of the two approaches proposed: on the one hand, *maintenance* (of the mother tongue in the educational system) calls for a cultural pluralism and linguistic diversity; on the other hand, *transitional* (mother tongue use in the educational system) calls for social and cultural homogeneity with minority assimilation and language shift.

Most government policies around the world are promoting a widespread impression that bilingualism (or multilingualism) is an uncommon linguistic phenomenon. D. Crystal (2002, P.366) appears highly critical about such attitudes. The author's feeling is that:

Language, sooner or later, proves to be a thorn in the flesh of all who govern, whether at national or local level. Different social groups wish to see their linguistic identities and interests maintained, and may actively-and often violently-campaign for recognition.

The point is that promoting the converse impression involves governments to undertake the huge task of designing policies and to plan the recognised languages. The task requires the search for significant funds which may not be readily available. That is why most multilingual countries recognise only very few languages among the very many that they actually have.

Like most Sub-Saharan African countries, Mali is a bilingual/multilingual nation with several native languages, thirteen of which have been elevated to the status of national languages and used in elementary school as media of education. The Malian educational system allows the use of French in its classical schools as the sole medium of education, and French coupled with a national language in its bilingual schools (Convergent Pedagogy and later Curriculum schools).

While there are several typologies of bilingual education planning (T. Skutnabb-Kangas, 1981, pp. 121-125), this research focuses on three basic ones which are discussed in the lines below.

Mackey's Typology

This typology is discussed in four different dimensions which can be crosstabulated to produce 90 possibilities.

First dimension: When discussing the relationship between the language(s) of the home and that of the school, Mackey makes a distinction between learners from unilingual and bilingual homes, with the home language (one or both) used or not used as school language.

Second dimension (curriculum): Mackey distinguishes between (1) medium of instruction (single or dual medium), (2) pattern of development (maintenance of two or more languages or transfer from one medium of education to another), (3) distribution of the languages (different, equal or the same), (4) direction (towards assimilation [acculturation] into a dominant culture or towards integration into a resurgent one, i.e. irredentism), and (5) complete or gradual change from one medium to another.

Third dimension: It is the linguistic character of the immediate environment as compared with the wider national environment. He uses a model of four different circles, each of which takes in a larger area than the previous one. His scheme of expansion is from the home, to the school, to the immediate environment or region, and finally to the whole country, the nation. All ten of his curriculum types can be placed in the school category, and these can be set beside the nine varieties of environmental pattern he distinguishes (according to whether each circle is mono or bilingual and whether the languages in all of them are the same or different), to give us 10 x 9 possible combinations.

4

Fourth dimension: It has to do with the function of the languages, their status as regional, national or international languages, and with differences between the languages, but since he does not use this dimension to expand the typology, they will not be dealt with here. It is obviously difficult to try to typologize bilingual education in such a comprehensive way as Mackey has attempted.

Fishman's Typology

It deals with some bilingual educational aspects which are missing from Mackey's curriculum types. It involves four types.

Type I (transitional bilingualism):

It envisages a scheme in which the minority language is used only during the first few years of schooling and then only in so far as it is needed to help the children to adapt to school life and /or to learn their various subjects until their knowledge of English [the majority language] is good enough to allow it to be used as the language of instruction (T. Skutnabb-Kangas, 1981, pp. 124).

Type II (monoliterate bilingualism or literacy in only one of the languages): it aims at developing children's oral proficiency in both languages, but no attempt is made to help them develop literacy skills in their own mother tongue, but in the majority language.

Type III (partial bilingualism): it aims to develop in children a fluent command of both languages, also in reading and writing, but with only a few subjects actually taught in the children's mother tongue because of their particular significance to the children's ethnic group and its cultural heritage.

Type IV (complete bilingualism): it encourages the children to develop both languages in all functions and domains, thus without any kind of diglossia. Both languages are generally used as subject teaching media, the aim being to maintain and develop the minority language. Fishman's typology heavily rests on the assumption that any particular programme is best judged by its aim, making by the same token, the distinction between the organization and the aim of a programme, which Mackey does not make.

Gonzáles' Typology

In his classification of different types of bilingual educational programme, J. M. Gonzáles uses a sliding scale. In his typology, too, the most important criterion of any scheme is its aim, but he assesses even more clearly than Fishman the extent to which any particular programme serves the interest of the minority. Moreover, his various types of programme cover a broader area than Fishman's.

Type A. English as a foreign language/bilingual (transitional): this has a strictly compensatory orientation.

Type B. Bilingual maintaining: the children's proficiency in another language is seen as a positive element, worth maintaining and developing.

Type C. Bilingual/bicultural (maintaining): while it resembles Type B, it also integrates the target group's *history and culture* as part and parcel of the content and methodology of the curriculum.

Type D. Bilingual/bicultural (restoring): it makes a serious attempt to give the children an opportunity to learn the language and culture of their ancestors, knowledge of both of which may have been lost in the process of assimilation.

Type E. Culturally pluralist: the children are not subject to any restriction based on the linguistic group they belong to. They all take part in linguistically and culturally pluralist education. Gonzales does not want his types of programme aimed only at certain restricted groups; rather he wants all schoolchildren, both minority and majority, to become multilingual and multicultural and that is an idealistic utopia.

Fishman's Typology of bilingual education planning fits best the Malian context. It implies that the native language (coupled with French) is taught and used as a medium of education for the first six years of schooling; during that period, there is a transition from the mother tongue to the main language of education (French). Starting from the seventh grade, the mother tongue is dropped, and the child continues with French. Therefore, this study focuses on the use of a national language concomitantly with French as media of education from grade one to grade six and even beyond as proposed by the new education orientation programme.

Admittedly, the use of French as the only medium of education at school has resulted into huge school drop-outs and unemployment; that is why successive governments in Mali have decided to opt for bilingual education (at least partially) in basic education, with the conviction that it will solve most of the problems that currently plague the educational system in the country.

At the sociolinguistic level, attitude study has been the concern of several researchers who sometimes differently perceive the concept. There are generally two main competing theoretical approaches to language attitude study: the behaviourist and the mentalist (R. Appel and P. C. Muysken, 1987, p.16). The behaviourist theory perceives and explains attitudes in terms of their actual use in communicative interaction and has just a communicative component. A proponent of this theory is R. Fasold (1984, pp.147-48) who conceives attitudes as the reactions that people display in social situations.

The mentalist theory considers attitudes as an inner mental state or disposition that may be conducive to overt behaviour. In the words of Allport (1935) cited in R. Agheyisi and J. A. Fishman (1970, p.138) attitudes are a *"mental and neural state of readiness"* that can ensure helpful insights into how people perceive themselves in relation to social phenomena (C. D. W. Robinson, 1991, p.240). In this paradigm, attitudes are seen as psychological constructs (C. Baker, 1992, p.16) and have to be inferred from the subject's introspection (R. Agheyisi and J. A. Fishman, 1970, p.138). Most attitude studies rely on the mentalist approach (Appel and Muysken, 1987; C. Baker, 1992; Bosch and De-Klerk, 1996; Cargile and Giles, 1998; El-Dash and Busnardo, 2001; Hoare and Coveney, 2000; Ioratim-Uba, 1995; Long, 1999; Payne, Downing and Fleming, 2000; and Pieras, 2000).

C. Baker (1992, p.12) prefers to make a combination of the behaviourist and the mentalist theories and to come up with the following three components: cognitive (pertaining to thoughts and beliefs), affective (relating to feelings) and readiness for action (concerning behavioural action plan under specific contexts or circumstances). This theoretical combination can help explain the attitudes and beliefs reported by Songhay users and their true linguistic behaviours in concrete social settings.

U. Smit (1996) suggests that when investigating language attitudes, the specifities of the nature of multilingual communities should be accounted for. J. Edwards (1994, p.34) points out that *"multilingualism is largely a practical affair"* and *"few people become or remain multilingual on a whim"*.

H. R. Giles, Y. Bourhis and D. M. Taylor's (1977) Theory of Language in Ethnic-group Relations appears particularly useful in determiningg why attitudes are formed as a result of those relations. The theory sees language as one of the principal bases for categorising people into social groups. Language in intergroup contexts may represent in-group inclusion or solidarity or out-group exclusion. Inferior or subordinate group members usually have negative perceptions about their language (variety or style). J. Edwards (1994), in the same vein, considers that in a multilingual area, the high-status language or language variety group is often positively perceived by the in-group and out-group (lower-status) members; that of the lower-status group is often negatively perceived by either group (P. Aziakpono and I. Bekker, 2010, p.41).

In inter-group comparison, language holds an important function in that the significance of the language of a group seen as a symbol of group identity appears highly crucial when the in-group is compared to the other groups. Members of a lower group who through intergroup comparison, perceive options to the prevailing situation generally embark on linguistic strategies to improve their social identity. The consequence at the individual level will be social mobility that often involves the adoption of the high-status language or variety, while at the group level, there will be the alternatives of assimilation and redefinition of negative characteristics that respectively involve the shift of a whole subordinate group to the language of the dominant or a re-evaluation of the language of the group in a more positive light. That re-evaluation may inspire in the relevant language variety and positive attitudes towards it (Giles et al, 1977). In the same vein, Songhay speakers of Gao may want to shift from Songhay to French in that they do not want their children to be in a bilingual Songhay-French-based system, but rather, in a French only-based one because French is seen as a high-status language. Therefore, they may want to upgrade their social and economic status and integrate the users of the French language. This does not mean that they do not like their Songhay mother tongue, but they have come to develop a better image of French and its users because of the political, social and economic benefits related to the mastery and use of that language: former colonial languages in Africa generally symbolise power, and s/he who masters them masters social, political and economic power. Therefore, as adopted by C. Baker (1992), this research is grounded on a combination of the mentalist and the behaviourist language attitude theories, with a special attention paid to H. R. Giles, Y. Bourhis and D. M. Taylor's 1977 Theory of Language in Ethnic-group Relations.

0.1. Importance and need for native language-based education

Bilingual Education (known in the Malian context as Convergent Pedagogy and its later development, the Curriculum) is a pedagogical innovation which is based on education in both the mother tongue and the official language, French. W Grabe and R. B. Kaplan (1992, p.221) citing R. F. Macias support that:

> More recent research indicates that greater school success and cognitive benefits are derived from initial native-language literacy instruction, and that there is a sequential transfer to literacy in a second language; the findings of their research argue for coherent programs of instruction in biliteracy.

The mother tongue, as indicated above, is that language acquired naturally and unconsciously in early infancy. The child is now embarking on making sense of his social milieu in his mother tongue; later on, he will be expected to make a smooth transfer of skills from the mother tongue to the second language in which formal education will continue. It is good to underline the high significance of mother based education in learning scientific disciplines such as arithmetic, physics, chemistry, etc. That is why a number of African countries (Rwanda, Madagascar, Algeria, Niger, Burkina Faso, to cite just a few) are struggling hard to implement such kind of policies.

Mother tongue instruction becomes very salient with decentralisation and the emergence of community schools all over the country. Such proximity schools need teachers who are generally recruited from the school drop-outs of the area. These people who were excluded by a school system based on the teaching from scratch of all the subjects in French, become now key components in the new system.

In decentralisation, there are a numerous concepts that communities do not easily grasp in French, but they come to easily comprehend in their mother tongue as such concepts were already taught and learnt at school through the new methodology. That is why the seminar on the domains and conditions of use of the national languages required a certificate in a national language whenever possible.

The same holds true with justice that would come closer to the community as no translation from mother tongue (L1) to second/foreign language (L2) or vice-versa would be required. Much of the court terminology would be taught and learnt at school in the mother tongue. The community would no longer get the feeling that justice is an external force imposed upon it, but would rather take ownership of it. Here again the seminar proposed the translation and the diffusion of the law in the national languages and the use of the national languages in a court of law.

In the civil service, it has been recommended to take into account the national languages as subjects in competitions, the translation of official documents, including identity cards and birth certificates into the national languages (Mali, Ministère de l'Education Nationale, 1999, p.6). In the work place, the mother tongues could be ascribed the same status as the official language. Both languages can equally be used. In terms of health care, both doctors and patients would make less effort in understanding instructions, information, awareness-raisng, sanitation, etc., if everybody used the same tongue. In short, a major advantage to bilingual education is that it tends to fill up the gap separating the illiterate from literate communities.

0.2. Overview of native language use in education

When Mali became independent in 1960, only 7% of its population could read and write (S. Traoré, 2001, p.4). The new government quickly undertook a system of mass and quality education. The results achieved were somewhat poor. The Education Reform of 1962 was meant to solve this state of illiteracy by advocating the use of native languages in education as

9

soon as the conditions would allow (ibid). The assumption behind this policy was that language is the main instrument of development, and no country could be developed through a foreign language. Education should therefore begin with/and in the mother tongue for the child is at ease in his mother tongue as when he is in the hands of his mother, and in denying him the possibility of using the familiar linguistic support which can meet his basic need of expression and creativity, the school by the same token, puts him in a situation of regression (J. Poth, 1988).

One salient impetus which further encouraged the Malian government in this direction came from the Conference of the Education Ministers held in Teheran in 1965, which proposed a new orientation for education in the world: mother tongue-based adult functional literacy. A further impetus came from a more recent conference, the *World Conference* on *'Education For All' (EFA)* of March 1990, held in Jomtien in Thailand, which especially pledged to work towards making basic education available for everyone. The concern was therefore to include even disadvantaged groups such as the poor, women and girls, and ethnic minorities. The Conference adopted the *World Charter on Education For All* and the *Action Framework to Meet Education Needs* (Mali, Ministère de l'Education, PRODEC, 2002, p.6). Of course, Jomtien was not the only education conference held in this perspective. The first conference can be traced back to May 1961 in Addis Ababa where African Education Ministers gathered "... *to initiate a drive that would facilitate universal primary education within a decade"*, (Mali, Ministère de l'Education Nationale, 1995, p.104). Three years later, in 1964, the Abidjan meeting was held in order to assess the work done since Addis Ababa and to propose new perspectives. The conference of Nairobi (1968) put stress on adapting school to the learner's social milieu through the use of the native languages and rural work. Lagos (1976) attempted to strengthen the achievements of the previous meetings by bringing *"innovations into education and basic education in the service of development"* (ibid). Harare (1982) only analysed the situation from Addis Ababa to Lagos and noticed that progress was not made. A further conference to note in this perspective is that of Dakar (1991), held a year after Jomtien. The meeting examined two major issues: increased access to basic education and the improvement in education quality. The conference made recommendations pertaining to sub-regional co-operation in education, curricula reform, and teacher pre- and in-service training. The last of these conferences was organised from March 28th to 31st 1995 in Ségou, on the initiative of the government of Mali.

This analysis shows how highly aware were the African political leaders correlation between education and development. That was obviated in the meeting of Nairobi which

10

called for the use of the native languages in education in order to gear training to the learner's social environment. But the question to ask is, How do Africans perceive mother tongue-based education? In other words, do they perceive training in the native languages as education?

In fact, most Africans perceive education as learning in/a foreign language, i.e., the acquisition of skills which the majority of the population does not have (elitism). In Mali, the use of French as a medium of education has resulted in huge failure: rate of school drop-outs (15.6%), class repetition (28.8%), high rate of exclusion, and a psychological blockage on the part of the learner (M. M. Konaté and P. Tamboura, (1999, p.17). The point to make here is that language usually stands as the vehicle for social and cultural values. The use of a foreign language such as French implies the inculcation in the learner of the French social and cultural values, at the expense of the learner's own values, disconnecting him, by the same token, from his own social milieu. It has equally been noted that pupils who use French as their medium of education are faced with a double task: they have to cope with the new language they are exposed to; they also have to cope with the acquisition of knowledge in that language. The bilingual pupils face only one task, that of learning science.

Relying on the above-mentioned statistics, and taking into account the results achieved by the functional literacy programmes in the national languages, the Second National Seminar on Education held in Bamako (Mali) in December 1978 recommended, inter alia, the experimentation of the local languages in formal education. Four major objectives were set:

i)   to achieve greater integration between school and the social milieu of the learner;

ii)   to facilitate the learning of instrumental subjects such as reading, writing, and mathematics),

iii)   to improve the internal output of the educational system, and

iv)   to increase the value of the national languages and culture.

The first four experimental schools were opened in 1979 in Kossa and N'Djifina in the region of Koulikoro, and Banankoroni and Zanabougou in the region of Ségou (Y. Mariko, 1993, p.24). These schools formed what is known in Convergent Pedagogy as the *First Generation* (Y. Haidara, 1998, p.11). The first language to be experimented was Bamanakan.

The results achieved by the experimental schools not only demonstrated that the new methodology could be effective, but also that it could solve most of the challenges facing education. In fact, while 53 pupils (46.08%) out of 115 (1979-1980) from the experimental schools of Banankoroni and Zanabougou reached the 6th form (June 1985) without repeating any class, only 24 pupils (7.05%) out 340 from the classical schools (Group I, II and III) reached the 6th form without repeating any class (Mali, Ministère de l'Education de Base, 1998, p.8). And while 22.57% of the experimental school pupils successfully passed the 7th grade entrance test, only 4.11% of the classical school pupils successfully passed the same test.

The experience accumulated from the experimentation and the results achieved led to the introduction, in 1982, of three more languages, viz. Fulfuldé in Mopti, Songhay and Tamasheq in Gao, Timbuktu, and Kidal.

The *Second Generation* started in 1987 with teaching in the native languages and French. The first two experimental schools were opened in Ségou. It is significant to note that the basic difference between the experimental schools and the classical ones was up to then the medium of education: experimental schools used native languages concomittantly with French, starting from 1987, while classical schools used French only. Convergent Pedagogy, as the methodology came to be called had been in generalisation since October 1994, but because of weaknesses uncovered in its implementation, it has been replaced by the Curriculum approach.

The Curriculum is nothing more than a new educational curriculum strongly based on convergent pedagogy, but presenting significant differences on different grades:

i)   it heavily relies on the use of native tongues as media of education at school;

ii)   the timetables are structured;

iii)   the subjects to teach are specified;

iv)   the subjects are grouped into domains (SH, SMT, LC, etc);

v)   the time devoted to each subject has been determined.

C. Baker (1988, p.112) expresses the significance of attitudes when he asserts, *"the success of language policy is partly predicated on attitudes surrounding that language"*. As to E. G. Lewis (1981, p.262) cited in C. Baker (1988, p.112) he observes that:

> *Any policy for language, especially in the system of education, has to take account of the attitude of those likely to be affected. In the long run, no policy, which does not do one of three things, will succeed: conform to the expressed attitudes of those involved; persuade those who express negative attitudes about the rightness of the policy; or seek to remove the causes of disagreement.*

That is all the more true that attitude knowledge helps understand the degree of success or failure of a language programme or planning and determine how to remedy.

D. Crystal (2003, p.256) describes language attitudes as:

12

The feelings people have about their own language or the language(s) of others. These may be positive or negative: someone may particularly value a foreign language [e.g. because of its literary history] or think that a language is especially difficult to learn [e.g. because the script is off-putting].

Joining C. Baker (1988), D. Crystal (2003) stresses further the great importance that should be ascribed to attitude knowledge and posits that *"knowing about attitudes is an important aspect of evaluating the likely success of a language teaching programme or a piece of language planning"* (ibid).

Still in the same direction, H. F. Schiffman (1997, p.4) underlines the great importance which should be given to attitude studies in policy design and maintains that:

They may affect the implementation of policy and cause it to fail. Or results may be obtained that are not anticipated or predicted, THE LAW OF UNINTENDED CONSEQUENCES, resources may be wasted, no changes result, with perhaps even superficial relationships.

0.3. Objectives, hypotheses and significance of the study

The current study investigates the attitudes of people in the urban commune of Gao towards Songhay as a medium of education for their children at school. It specifically aims to determine i) the nature (types) of attitudes that people have about the use of their own mother tongue, Songhay, as a language of education for their children at school; ii) to comprehend the nature (types) of attitudes that they have about the use of French as a medium of education for their children at school; iii) to develop strategies to motivate parents to send their children to mother tongue-based schools; and v) to use the results of the study to better raise the awareness of people on the necessity to participate in the reinforcement of the use of bilingual education to quicken community development.

To implement the research, two main hypotheses have been designed. K. F. Punch (2005, p.38) defines a hypothesis:

As a predicted answer to a research question. To say we have a hypothesis is to say we can predict what we will find in answer to a question. We make this prediction before we carry out the research-a priori. A specific research question states what we are trying to find out. The hypothesis predicts a priori the answer to that question.

The hypotheses have been formulated as follows:

i)   People in the commune of Gao have positive attitudes towards the use of Songhay as a medium of education for their children at school;

ii)   People in the commune of Gao have negative attitudes towards the use of Songhay as a medium of education for their children at school.

The need for such a study lies in the assumption that no country can develop in a foreign language, but only in the native language(s). While several studies (S. Traoré (2001), Y. Haidara (2004), M. M. Konaté and P. Tamboura (1999), etc. have been carried out on mother tongue-based education, very few have tackled the issue of the *attitudes* of those who send their children to school, or the attitudes of the children themselves and of the other school partners. M. Minkailou (2017a) finds that most school actors reject the bilingual system and advocate the classical French-based one. The reasons behind such feelings are that the mastery and use of French ensures social, economic, political and financial benefits that Songhay cannot provide. French tends to mean political power. A less related study, still on attitudes, is M. Minkailou (2017b) which focuses on attitudes and language shift (from Mamara to Bamanankan): Minianka people in Mali tend to have a low image of themselves and their Mamara mother tongue, give up that language and shift to Bamanankan which they find more prestigious and economically more powerful. This implies that even in terms of bilingual education, Minianka people would advocate a Bamanankan-French combination for their children, rather than a Mamara-French one. M. L. Haidara (1990, p.33) describes parents' perception about the method in the Pedagogical Animation Centre of Ségou I. The study reveals that 63.8% of parents value the national languages and have favourable perception about them. The study also demonstrates that while some parents send their children to bilingual experimental schools because they have no alternatives (there are no classical schools nearby) most of them feel satisfied with the results. An earlier work by the same author analysed the attitudes of teachers towards the introduction of national languages in schools in Bamako.

Y. Mariko (1993, p.p27-38) focuses on parents' attitudes toward the introduction of national languages into the educational system. The study concludes that while some worries are expressed, the majority of parents are in favour of the innovation. The results of this study correlates with those of the first experimental studies which showed that parents were unfavourable at the beginning of the process but that they accepted the approach because they thought they could not do otherwise. However, when they perceived the positive results (100% admission rate by the pupils of the school of Banakoroni in the region of Ségou in 1985) achieved by their children, they all became favourable. Several Bachelor level theses have been devoted to the introduction and use of mother tobgue-based education. However, no research is known to have taken place on how Songhay people feel about the use of their

Songhay mother tongue as a medium of education for their children at school. More, no serious study is known to have taken place on attitudes towards the use of native languages as media of education at school. Therefore, this research has been conducted to fill up that gap.

Chapter one: The methodological procedures

The present study is a self-report or descriptive method-based investigation. The researcher's decision to use this method stems from the fact that his hypotheses can only be best elicited by a descriptive approach, the most appropriate research tool to measure attitudes. In this sense, a questionnaire was designed and addressed to a random sample of eighteen (18) teachers and two (2) school headmasters. And in order to triangulate, the researcher finds it more appropriate (in terms of validity and reliability) to balance the data collected via the questionnaire by data collected via the interview. That is why the questionnaire has been coupled with an interview with a sample of twenty-nine (29) pupils, five (5) Parent Teacher Association (PTA) members, nine (9) members of the School Management Committee (SMC), three (3) members of the Child Mother Association (CMA), (30) laymen and two (2) representatives of NGOs (Oxfam and World Education) working in the sector of education, making a total of 98 subjects.

Expectedly, both tools have their strengths and weaknesses. The questionnaire gives time and freedom of thinking to the respondent and frees him from psychological pressure, while at the same time it deprives him of the possibility of asking for clarifications about issues he might not understand. The interview, on the other hand, gives the respondent the possibility of understanding every item put because of the presence of the researcher or his assistant, but that same presence of the interviewer might have a negative impact on the interviewee.

Regarding the interview, the questions to ask have been printed on a form; but the interviewer keeps a tape recorder, and written records, with the permission of the interviewee, of everything that has been said. Then, the interview papers and tapes are assembled and analyzed in the same conditions as the questionnaire papers. It is significant to indicate here that the interview is structured: all the questions are closed with limited options presented on the respondent.

The carrying out of this research has required three field-trips to the research site, Gao: the first trip aimed at visiting and understanding the setting for the study; the second aimed at testing the research tools to determine how valid and reliable they are and to make corrections as necessary; the third aimed to administer the questionnaire and interview the informants.

1.1. The research setting

The site for the study is the urban commune of Gao (also known as Askia's City). The study took place in the districts of Gaday, Faranjiray and Julabugu. In order to have a balanced representativity of the different sections of the population, the study went from the suburban (Gaday), the semi-suburban (Faranjiray) and to the urban (Julabugu) districts of the city.

Gao being a Songhay stronghold, the majority of its population (68.26%) belongs to the Songhay ethnic group. The rest of the population is made up of Tuareg people speaking Tamasheq, Fulah people who, in most cases, have lost their Fulfulde mother tongue in favour of Sognhay, and Arabs speaking the Hasaniya Arabic variety. But, in general, every resident of the city speaks Songhay, the lingua franca of Northern Mali.

Historically, the city was the Capital of the Songhay Empire. Gao had known four stages in its historical development; each stage was marked by the reign of a dynasty.

-The Kungorogosi dynasty ruled Gao from a period difficult to date to 670;

-The Dia dynasty ruled from 670 to 1325;

-The Sonni dynasty ruled from 1337 to 1493, and finally

-The Askia dynasty ruled from 1493 to the Morrocan invasion in 1591 (H. O. Maiga. 2006, p. 132-5).

At the turn of the 19th century, Gao was taken over by the French colonisers who imposed their educational system and their assimilationist language policy.

The commune was created in the very late years of the colonial period (1958) and was given the status of average, then full commune. It was headed by an appointed administrator-mayor assisted by an elected deliberating body.

The commune covers 38.5 square kilometres with an urbanised area of 1,375 acres. The city is located on the left bank of the Niger River at the crossroad of three national roads (NR): NR16 joins Sévaré to Gao; NR 17 joins Ansongo to Gao; and NR18 joins Bourem to Gao.

The commune is bordered to the North by commune Sonni Ali Ber, to the West and South by the commune of Gunzuray, and to the East by the communes of Tilemsi and N'šawaji. The commune has nine districts: Gaday, Faranjiray, Aljanabandia, Julabugu, Sanay, Sosokoyra, Château (a very big district with four sectors) and Bulgunje.

The economic activities of the commune are dominated by the primary sector, mainly agriculture, but also traditional cattle-raising and fishing (1.4%). The secondary sector is dominated by trade (and transportation) and handicrafts, while industrial units are absent. The tertiary sector is somewhat represented by several local and regional services (16.20%). Some of the NGOs present in the city include SEAD, World Education, OXFAM GB, TASSAGHT, Save the Children, etc. At the time of the investigation, the commune had:

-One public high school,

-Thirty-three primary schools;

-Four vocational training centres;

-Seven koranic schools (Medersa); and

-Three kindergarterns.

The investigation was conducted in the schools of Gaday A and Faranjiray B.

1.1.1. Gaday A School

Gaday A[1] is located in the second district of the Commune called *Gaday*. At its creation in October 1961, it was called the *Fundamental School of Gaday*. Then it became *Gooroom, Gao II*, and finally *Gaday*. From 1961 to 1964, it was just a primary school. And from 1964 to 1975, it acquired a junior high school component. In 1978, the school was divided into two school groups: *Gaday A* and *Gaday B*. A third group, *Gaday C* was created in 2003.

Gaday A has eight (8) teachers and three hundred and ninety seven (397) pupils. The table below presents the number of pupils per year and type of curriculum they follow:

Table N°1: Distribution of the pupils of Gaday A among the educational systems.

Grade	Number of pupils	Type of curriculum
1	103	Curriculum
2	54	Curriculum
3	37	Convergent Pedagogy
4 A	25	Convergent Pedagogy
4 B	24	Classical French-based
5 A	44	Classical French-based
5 B	50	Classical French-based
6	60	Classical French-based
Total	397	

The school is run by a School Management Committee (SMC), the Parent Teacher Association (PTA) and the Child Mother Association (CMA). There are eight (8) SMC members, two (2) CMA members, but an unknown number of PTA members.

1.1.2. Faranjiray B School

The school is located in the third district of the commune, Franjiray. Initially, there was just *the School of Faranjiray*, created in 1905. It was the first school of the region and used legionnaires as teachers. In 1925, it became the regional school and was transferred from the

---

[1] Information contained in this section comes from the head teacher's files.

Military Barrack where it had been since its creation, to the place of the present Vegetable Market in 1925, and finally to its present site on January 1st 1955. It started with six (6) grades, then seven (7) and finally nine (9). In 1966, it started its junior high school section called *Gao III*, and in January 1969, was transferred to Julabugu (Gao V). On October 1st 1972, the school of Faranjiray was divided into *Faranjiray A* and *Faranjiray B*. Two years later, a third school, *Faranjiray C*, was created.

Faranjiray B has thirteen (13) teachers and three hundred and thirty four (334) pupils. The table below presents the six grades in the school, the number of pupils and the curriculum type followed.

Table N°2: Distribution of the pupils of Faranjiray B among the educational systems.

Grade	Number of pupils	Type of curriculum
1	64	Curriculum
2	72	Curriculum
3	75	Convergent Pedagogy
4	56	Convergent Pedagogy
5	38	Convergent Pedagogy
6	29	Convergent Pedagogy
Total	334	

Like *Gaday A*, *Faranjiray B* too was run by a SMC, a PTA and a CMA. There were eleven (11) PTA members, seven (7) SMC members and seven (7) CMA members.

1.2. Description of the sample

This section presents the characteristics of the subjects in the study, namely, the headmasters, the teachers, the pupils, the laymen, the NGO representatives, and the PTA, CMA and SMC members.

1.2.1. Headmasters

They are two experienced informants (53 and 54 years old); both are married. The number of years spent in their position (10 and 32 years) indicates that they should know about the issue of language and education in Mali. According to the headmaster of Faranjiray B, his school was the first in the entire region to have joined Convergent Pedagogy in 1994-1995, while Gaday A, the other school in the study, had to wait nine years later to embrace Convergent Pedagogy. But both schools introduced the Curriculum Approach the same year (2005). Both respondents belong to the Songhay community of the commune of Gao. The table below sums-up their characteristics:

Table N°3: Characteristics of the headmasters

	Age of headmaster	Married		Number of years in position	School	Beginning of bilingual education	
		yes	No			Convergent Pedagogy	Curriculum
DFB[2]	54	x		32	Faranjiray B	1994	2005
DGA[3]	53	x		10	Gaday A	2003	2005

While the significance of the headmaster population lies in the fact that they are the people who follow the implementation of the new methodology, that of the teachers' population lies in the fact that they are the classroom practitioners who implement the innovation. The next section describes the characteristics of the teacher subjects.

1.2.2. Teachers

The teacher group is made up of two sub-groups. On the one hand, there is the classical teacher sub-group that is composed of four (4) people. On the other hand, there is the bilingual teacher group, made up of fourteen (14) people.

1.2.2.1. Classical French-based teachers

At this level, the number of teachers is smaller because the classical system it represents is in decline in favour of bilingual education. Strikingly, they all come from Gaday A, one of the last schools of the Commune to have introduced bilingual education. The sub-group displays characteristics which are presented in the table below.

Table N°4: Characteristics of the classical French-based teachers.

Teachers' ID	Age of teacher	Married		Number of children	Teaching experience
		Yes	no		
FTGA[4]1	37	X		2	6
FTGA2	31	X		2	9
FTGA3	37	X		1	10
FTGA4	34	X		4	9

---

[2] Director of Faranjiray B.
[3] Director of Gaday A.
[4] **FTGA** stands for **F**rench (classical system) **T**eacher in **G**aday **A**.

The table shows that there is a single age group which ranges from thirty-one to thirty-seven. They look more or less experienced (between six and ten years) in education. They also have fewer children who might not have school age.

1.2.2.2. Bilingual teachers

This second teacher group is larger because the bilingual system it represents is in expansion at the expense of the classical one. The group is made up of fourteen (14) subjects who come from the two target schools and who display characteristics that are depicted in the table below:

Table N°5: Characteristics of the bilingual teachers.

Teachers' ID	Age of teacher	Married Yes	No	Number of children	Teaching experience	Bilingual teaching experience
STGA[5]1	?	x		5	26	4
STGA2	36	x		1	5	1
STGA3	34	x		?	?	?
STGA4	48	x		6	23	3
STFB[6]1	?	x		2	5	1
STFB2	43	x		3	14	10
STFB3	28		X	0	4	3
STFB4	30	x		0	5	5
STFB5	42	x		6	20	5
STFB6	54	x		8	30	21
STFB7	42	x		4	6	6
STFB8	30	x		2	4	4
STFB9	30		X	1	4	4
STFB10	42	x		3	16	10

There are two teacher age groups:

-Twenty eight (28) to thirty six (36): they are six subjects four of whom are at least thirty years old. The group seems less experienced and is composed of non permanent teachers. Their experience ranges from four years (including three years spent in the bilingual system) to five years (including four years spent in the bilingual system).

-Forty two (42) to fifty four (54): they are six informants who are all civil servants. Their experience ranges from fourteen (14) years (including ten years spent in the bilingual system) to thirty (30) years (including twenty one years spent in the bilingual system). The one

---

[5] **STGA:** **S**onghay **T**eacher of **G**aday **A**
[6] **STFB:** **S**onghay **T**eacher of **F**aranjiray **B**

21

respondent who has spent twenty-one years in bilingual education must have started since the period of experimental schools (1979 and 1987). Two (2) subjects are are not married, and two (including one among the unmarried ones) do not have children. Seven people among these informants have at least three children, the maximum number being eight children. It should nevertheless be signalled that Songhay people do not really like to be asked questions about their age and the number of children they have. And when they feel obliged to answer such questions, they may just give false figures, usually lower than the correct ones. So the figures regarding the number of children in this research should be taken with caution.

The importance of describing the subjects in the study has already been noted. The pupils make no exception. So the next section is devoted to the description of the characteristics of the pupils of the selected schools.

1.2.3. Pupils

Like the teachers, the pupils are composed of two (2) groups: one classical and the other bilingual. They have all been selected according to specific criteria.

1.2.3.1. Classical French-based pupils

The pupil subjects come from Gaday A. Their number is low because of the extension of the bilingual system at the expense of the classical one. The sub-group is made up of eight (8) pupils described in the table below:

Table N°6: Characteristics of the classical French-based pupils.

Pupils' ID	Age of pupil	Grade	Number of times classes are repeated	Father's occupation
FPGA[7]1	15	5	3	Blacksmith
FPGA2	13	5	1	Teacher
FPGA3	17	5	2	Driver
FPGA4	13	5	1	Passed away
FPGA5	15	5	1	Blacksmith
FPGA6	11	5	1	Welder
FPGA7	14	5	0	Trader
FPGA8	13	5	1	Welder

---

[7] *FPGA:*French Pupils of Gaday *A.*

22

The data in the table above show that the respondents' age varies between eleven (11) and seventeen (17). The age groups are as follows:
- Eleven (11) to twelve (12): one student;
- Thirteen (13) to fifteen (15): six students.
- Seventeen (17) and more: one student.

The age groups presented in the table indicate that the majority of the pupils went to school between 1999 and 2000. At that time, Convergent Pedagogy and the Curriculum had not started in Gaday A. So, parents indistinctly sent their children to school.

All these pupils are from the fifth grade of Gaday A. In other words, the first and third grades of Gaday A follow a bilingual program, and the selected subjects from that school will be found in the bilingual group.

In terms of performance, two subjects who might be slow learners, have repeated twice or three times classes; five have repeated one class; and one has repeated no class.

The occupations of the pupils' fathers are various: there are two blacksmiths, two welders, one teacher, one driver and one trader. So the majority of the pupils' parents seem to be illiterate people who did not know about bilingual education, and who just sent their children to school.

1.2.3.2. Bilingual pupils

This group is made up of twenty-one (21) subjects. Eight (8) come from Gaday A and thirteen (13) from Faranjiray B. Their characteristics are portrayed in the table below.

Table N°7: Description of the bilingual pupils.

Pupils' ID	Age of pupil	Grade	Number of times classes are repeated	Father's occupation
SPGA[8]1	12	3	1	City hall worker
SPGA2	10	3	1	Trader
SPGA3	10	3	1	SOTELMA worker
SPGA4	8	1	0	Farmer
SPGA5	7	1	1	Trader
SPGA6	7	1	0	Farmer
SPGA7	7	1	1	Trader
SPGA8	7	1	0	Video player
SPFB[9]1	8	2	0	City hall worker
SPFB2	10	2	2	Traditional healer
SPFB3	10	2	1	Radio repairer
SPFB4	11	2	1	Necklace seller
SPFB5	11	2	0	Constructor worker
SPFB6	9	2	1	Koranic teacher
SPFB7	10	2	0	City hall worker
SPFB8	14	4	1	Tailor
SPFB9	14	4	1	Mechanic
SPFB10	14	4	1	Driver
SPFB11	12	4	1	Gas seller
SSFB12	14	6	0	Deceased
SPFB13	14	6	0	Deceased

A close look at the above table discloses the following information:

-1st grade pupils: they are four (4), and their age ranges from seven to eight;

- 2nd grade pupils: they are seven (7), and the age ranges from eight to eleven;

- 3rd grade pupils: they are three (3), and the age ranges from ten to twelve;

- 4th grade pupils: they are four (4), and the age ranges from twelve to fourteen;

---

[8]*SPGA*: *S*onghay *P*upils of *G*aday *A*.

[9] *SPFB:S*onghay *P*upils of *F*aranjiray *B*.

- 5th grade pupils: 0 (zero). There are no fifth form pupils (because they follow a classical programme);
- 6th grade pupils: they are two (2) and are fourteen (14) years old.

One significant point to highlight is that all the pupils (but one) have repeated once at the most. This implies that the performance level of the group is higher than that of the classical French-based pupils.

The fathers' occupations are diverse and include three (3) city hall workers, two (2) traders, two (2) farmers, one (1) SOTELMA worker, one (1) mechanic, one (1) repairer, etc. On the whole, four (4) informants' fathers out of twenty one (21) seem to be educated or at least literate.

Having presented the characteristics of the pupil subjects, the next section dedicated to the description of the representatives of SEAD and World Education.

1.2.4. Representatives of SEAD and World Education

There are several NGOs and technical and financial partners that work in Gao. But only two, namely, SEAD and World Education carry out activities in the field of education in the commune. Each of the two NGOs has an education specialist. For instance, at SEAD, there is a staff responsible for education matters; and at World Education, there is an assistant responsible for community participation in education. These two are the ones the researcher has interviewed. The table below sums-up their characteristics.

Table N°8: Characteristics of the representatives of SEAD and World Education.

| Name of NGO | Age of agent | Position | Number of years in position | Married | | Number of children |
				yes	no	
SEAD	41	Education responsible	19	x		6
World Education	44	Community Involvement Assistant	4	x		8

The data in the table uncovers that the two NGO representatives are adult education leaders who are aware of the current major educational concerns in the Commune. The representative of SEAD who appeared a little younger is nevertheless highly experienced since he has held his position for nineteen years, while the World Education representative who looks older has held his position for only four years. Both subjects are married and have school aged children.

A further group of subjects in this investigation is the members of SMC, PTA, and CMA whose characteristics are described in the upcoming section.

1.2.5. The School Management Committee, the Parent Teacher Association and the Child Mother Association.

There are sixteen (16) subjects split into three sub-groups:

1.2.5.1. The School Management Committee

They are eight (8) and include the president (Gaday A) and the general treasurer (Faranjiray B). Five members come from the school of Gaday A, and three from the school of Faranjiray B. The table below summarises their characteristics.

Table N°9: Characteristics of the School Management Committe.

SMC members' ID	Age of member	Married		Number of children	Occupation	Ethnic group
		yes	No			
SMCGA[10]1	53	x		8	School project responsible	Songhay
SMCGA2	69	x		7	Retired teacher	Fulah
SMCGA3	14		X	0	Pupil	Hausa
SMCGA4	52	x		6	Mentor	Songhay
SMCGA5	52	x		4	Housewife	Songhay
SMCGA6	31	x		2	Teacher	Songhay
SMCFB[11]1	43	x		3	Teacher	Songhay
SMCFB2	51	x		4	Teacher	Songhay
SMCFB3	42	x		4	Teacher	Songhay

They can be divided into two age groups:

-31-43: three subjects.

-51-69: five subjects.

---

[10] School Management Committee of Gaday **A.**
[11] School Management Committee of Faranjiray **B.**

26

The respondents are all married, and nearly all of them have school aged children. Only one of them is Fulah; the others are Songhay. Most of them are educated: five are teachers, one is a pupil, one is a mentor, and one is a housewife.

1.2.5.2. The Parent Teacher Association

They are five (5) members who also include the president of the central federation of the education sector of PTAs in the Cercle of Gao, who is also the president of the PTA of GadayA. Three (3) members come from Gaday A, and two (2) from Faranjiray B. All the members are married and have school aged children. Nearly all of them belong to the songhay ethnic group save for one who is Mossi.

Table N°10: Characteristics of the Parent Teacher Association.

PTA members ID	Age	Married		Number of children	Occupation	Ethnic group
		yes	no			
PTAGA[12]1	56	x		1	Retired teacher	Songhay
PTAGA2	46	x		3	Private school promoter	Songhay
PTAGA3	70	x		14	Retired teacher	Songhay
PTAFB[13]1	71	x		8	Retired lycée teacher	Songhay
PTAFB2	47	x		8	Laboratory assistant	Mossi

This table displays two age groups which go from middle to advanced age.

-46-56: they are three (3) subjects composed of two teachers and a laboratory assistant.

-70-71: they are two (2) retired teacher subjects.

1.2.5.3. The Child Mother Association

They are three (3) members: two (2) come from Faranjiray B, and one (1) from Gaday A.

---

[12] Parent Teacher Association of Gaday **A**.
[13] Parent Teacher Association of Faranjiray **B**.

Table N°11: Characteristics of the Child Mother Association.

CMA members' ID	Age	Married yes	Married no	Number children	Occupation	Ethnic group
CMAGA[14]1	60	x		8	Retired nurse	Songhay
CMAFB[15]1	41	x		6	Restaurant owner	Songhay
CMAFB2	53	x		7	Housewife	Fon (Benin)

The data in the table display two age groups which range from middle to advanced age:

-41: there is one (1) informant who is a restaurant owner with six children;

-53-60: there are two (2) informants; one is a housewife with seven and the other, a retired nurse with eight children. They are all married and have school aged children. Two (2) are Songhay and one (1) is a Beninese Fon.

1.2.6. Laymen

This group of rerspondents is made up of thirty (30) subjects the researcher has randomly selected either in families or in the streets for interview. The table below describes their characteristics.

---

[14] Child Mother Association of Gaday **A**.
[15] Child Mother Association of Faranjiray **B**.

Table N°12: Characteristics of the laymen.

Laymen's ID	Age	Married yes	no	Number of children	Occupation
LG[16]1	49	x		5	Tailor
LG2	39	x		3	Trader
LG3	38	x		4	Trader
LG4	40	x		4	Tailor
LJ5	?	x		2	Trader
LG5	48	x		8	Trader
LG6	47	x		7	Farmer
LG7	47	x		4	Joiner
LG8	53	x		?	Farmer
LG9	37	x		1	Driver
LG10	31	x		3	Farmer
LG11	17	x		1	Housewife
LG12	42	x		6	Imam
LF[17]1	46	x		4	Driver
LF2	39	x		2	Trader
LF3	50	x		3	Unemployed
LF4	27		x	0	Dyer
LF5	40	x		2	Trader and Farmer
LF6	33	x		2	Trader
LF7	37	x		2	Farmer
LF8	38	x		0	Farmer
LF9	37	x		0	Driver
LF10	35	x		0	Driver
LF11	75	x		8	Retired driver
LF12	69	x		7	Retired driver
LJ[18]1	32	x		1	Housewife
LJ2	70	x		1	Condiment seller
LJ3	67	x		6	Midwife
LJ4	53	x		7	Tailor
LJ6	43	x		3	Building technician

The informants have been classified into five (5) age groups described as follows:

[16] Layman of Gaday.
[17] Layman of Faranjiay.
[18] Layman of Julabugu.

-17: one (1) subject;

-30-40: fourteen (14) subjects;

-41-50: eight (8) subjects;

-51-60: two (2) subjects;

-61-75: four (4) subjects.

The informants are all married (save for one) and have all children (save for four). Their occupations are very diverse and are all unskilled jobs (like car driving). The subjects belong all to the Songhay ethnic group save for one who is a Miniyanka.

In short, the subjects targeted in this study are in the eyes of the researcher the true stakeholders of education in the commune of Gao. The description of their characteristics will help display their social, economic, and cultural conditions, and by the same token, those of their families. This information will help shed light on the subjects' responses and better comprehend and interpret those responses.

The proper study was preceded by a focus group investigation carried out in April 2005 in Gao, which gathered eight (8) informants from various occupations. The purpose of such an inquiry was to collect information, people's sentiments and ideas about the topic under investigation. That was followed by a pilot study which took place in March 2006 in Gaday, Faranjiray and Julabugu. Piloting was carried out in French or/and Songhay. During the field-trip for piloting, the researcher discovered that there were only two schools (Faranjiray C and Camps des Gardes Schools) which remained in the classical French-based system. All the other schools in the commune were mother tongue-based. But, the plain truth is that even Faranjiray C School was only officially bilingual, but classical French-based, in practice. As a result, only Camps des Gardes School was truly classical French-based.

The situation of Faranjiray C School was not an isolated case. Even the other schools which were said to be using Convergent Pedagogy were not really doing so: first, all the first grades (in some cases, even the second grades) were in a new pedagogical system called the 'Curriculum'; the remaining classes were either classical French-based, or were shared between French-based and Convergent Pedagogy and even the three systems. It was not rare to find a school where the three systems (Classical French system, Convergent Pedagogy, and Curriculum) were practiced. In Faranjiray A School for instance, the first grade was Curriculum, the second was Convergent Pedagogy, and the third, fourth, fifth and sixth grades were French-based. So the questionnaire was administered to teachers and head teachers according to whether they were using the Classical French-based system or Convergent Pedagogy/Curriculum. The same holds true with the interview which was conducted with pupils according to whether they were actually in a Classical French-based or a Convergent Pedagogy/Curriculum class.

It was not easy to get hold of PTA members. They only went to school when they were called upon or had something to do. The researcher was able to meet one member from the Classical French-based system and three others from the Convergent Pedagogy system. The number is low, but sufficient to test the validity and reliability of the research instruments. They were interviewed in French.

A major constraint that the researcher faced during the piloting phase was that he did not get permission from the school authorities to carry out the research in the area. That is why the headmaster of a school of Gaday refused to meet him and to let him interview the pupils. Another headmaster accepted, but at the end advised him to have permission next time he comes around.

The analysis of the results from the pilot study displayed the existence of complex questions in the pupils' interviews. Some pupils gave contradictory answers to questions; others simply conceded that they did not know how to answer some questions; this appears particularly true with the first and the second grade pupils, probably because of their younger age. Consequently, their interview items were revised and simplified. Moreover, all the interviews were translated into Songhay. In short, the work was refined.

The researcher also narrowed down the scope of the study by decreasing the number of schools in the sample, but compensated at the level of laymen and school partners (NGOs, etc.) Therefore, instead of four schools, the study has focused on two schools (Gaday A and Faranjiray B); and even then, criteria were used to identify the pupils and the classes to include in the study. All interviews of pupils, PTA members and laymen were translated into Songhay, duplicated and made available for the proper investigation.

As pointed out earlier, the purpose of piloting was to determine the extent to which the questionnaire to administer and the interview to carry out were sound, and to make adjustments as necessary. In this case, it is not so much the answers provided which were important; it is rather the extent to which the respondents clearly understood all the questions asked. That is why P. D. Leedy (1980, p.100) recommends that:

Every researcher should give the questionnaire to at least half a dozen of his friends, or neighbours, to test whether there are any items that they may have any difficulty in understanding or in comprehending exactly what the writer is seeking to determine.

In this sense, piloting serves the purpose of foretelling the researcher which questions are well/ill-formulated in order to provide the expected correct answers. Furthermore, it helps determine, foresee and limit possible constraints, difficulties and other problems, which the researcher might not perceive before the proper study begins.

1. 3. The study

The proper study started with Gaday A School. The first thing the researcher did was to get a written permission from the Pedagogical Animation Centre of Gao (the Inspectorate). Then, he got in touch with the research assistants who joined him. The headmasters' and the teachers' questionnaires were distributed and filled out in presence of the researcher who was able to help the respondents with the explanations of difficult items. Then, the copies were all collected. That was followed by the pupils' interviews which were conducted according to criteria already specified. The interviews focused on the 1st, 3rd, 5th A, and 5th B grades. Both the tape recorder and printed forms designed for that purpose were used.

The PTA members were contacted via the headmaster who indicated that they had not been taking part in their meetings for a very long time for unknown reasons. Nevertheless, the researcher was able to meet and interview their president (who is also the president of PTAs of the area and of the Cercle of Gao) and two other members. The rest of the group could not be contacted because neither the headmaster, nor the other members could help meet them. As to the members of SMC and CMA, they were invited to school by their presidents and the school headmaster; and they were all separately interviewed.

The work at Faranjiray B School began with a visit to the headmaster, followed by the distribution of the questionnaire, first to the headmaster, then to the teachers who were all gathered in a classroom. After receiving some explanations of the aims and some difficult items, the respondents all left the room to fill out the forms which they returned the next morning. The pupils' interview took place the same day with the 2nd, 4th, and 6th grades according to the criteria already established. Finally, the PTA, SMC and CMA members (including the president) were invited to school by the headmaster. Most of them accepted the invitation and came for the interview.

The remaining task to carry out was the interview of the thirty laymen in the three districts. The researcher started with the district of Gaday where twelve people were randomly selected for interview; he walked in the streets, stopped by people in street corners, and asked for permission to enter households for interview. This mainly happened in Julabugu, where people in the streets usually came from other districts for business. The researcher continued with the district of Faranjiray where twelve people were selected and interviewed, using the same strategy. He ended up with Julabugu where six people were selected for interview.

In most cases, the researcher was allowed to record the responses of the informants, but some people did not accept to have their voices recorded. It is also worth indicating that before each interview, permission was sought. And at the end of each interview, the researcher crosschecked all the answers on the spot before proceeding.

The interview of the NGO and financial and technical partners' representatives was the most difficult. First, the researcher had to meet all of them in order to understand the kinds of activities they were conducting and their areas of intervention. Only two NGOs (SEAD and World Education) were found to be working in the sector of education in the Commune. Their representatives were interviewed.

1.3.1. The questionnaire

In the present study, the type of questions used is the closed one, characterised by the limitations imposed upon the number of options proposed to the respondent in each item. C. Robson (1993, p.247) thinks that *"closed questions are usually preferable to open questions,"* though they are not always easy to design and though they do not always give freedom of response to the informant. Yet they are usually easier to analyse. The author also maintains that *"specific questions are better than general ones"* (ibid.) as they ensure greater standardisation. One main advantage of the self-completed questionnaire, as advocated in this study, is that it saves time and effort on the part of the researcher.

The questions all focus on people's attitudes towards Songhay as a language of education for their children in formal education. They aimed to understand the job opportunities mother tongue-based education can ensure, especially in the context of decentralisation, and the extent to which it can ensure the preservation of people's roots, identity and culture.

In terms of sampling procedures, the choice of the eight groups of informants stems from the fact that they are the people who are directly affected by language in education policy and planning. For instance, the bilingual teachers and the school headmasters are those who are in a better position to talk about the teaching practices, and their feelings about the issue are crucial in the degree students' success.

There are selection criteria for the schools and the classes:

-The school selection criterion: one school or the pupils attending it should come from the heart of the city (Faranjiray B). The other school, or the pupils attending it, should come from the suburb (Gaday A). The implementation of this first criterion has the advantage of giving a balanced view on what people in the commune think about mother tongue-based education.

-The class selection criterion: the school of Gaday A receives uneven classes: the first, third, and fifth grades. The school of Faranjiray B receives even classes: the second, fourth, and sixth grades.

1.3.2. The structured interview

There are at least three types of interviews at the disposal of a researcher. The first, formal or structured interview is a type in which the items are organised like a sequence of questions limited by the options provided. It does not allow flexibility in the answers to provide and is difficult to conceive, but allows easier data analysis. The second, the informal or unstructured interview, is quite the reverse of the formal type in that it provides the interviewee with full freedom to talk. It does not impose any constraints on the interviewee except those determined by the direction or the focus of the topic under study. The third type, the focused interview, is in between the first two. C. Robson (1993, p.240-1) citing an earlier study by Merton, Fiske, and Kendal (1956) describes it as *"an approach which allows people's views and feelings to emerge, but which gives the interviewer some control".*

Both the focused and the unstructured interview types tend to yield richer data. Yet, after a closer look at the strengths and weaknesses of each type of interview, it is the structured form that has been adopted in this survey.

In terms of sampling procedures, the interviewees' population is made up of the pupils, the PTA, SMC, CMA members, laymen and NGO representatives. They are the decision-makers about what parents want for their children; they also represent those parents in terms of feelings. As for the parents, they are the people who send their children to school and direct their education.

The pupils' selection criterion was in each selected grade of each selected school, the pupils were counted from one to ten and the tenth was selected for interview. The average number of pupils per class was around eighty.

Long before the interview day, all the subjects (except laymen) were informed of the researcher's intention of interviewing them at a date closed with, the data collection tools and eventually the future use of the responses. It is good to underline that though the data were directly collected on answer sheets made ready for the occasion, the use of the tape recorder helped secure all the collected information.

The researcher did not lose sight of the ethical issues surrounding the study. First, the researcher and his assistants are from the Songhay social milieu (born and raised in that milieu); they know the social and cultural values of songhay people. Therefore, in the formulation of the questions to put, the researcher has avoided asking 'distasteful' questions;

34

for instance, including items pertaining to the informants' names may result in growing in them the feeling that foreigners are spying on them. Informants have also been informed about the researcher and his assistants' identity (they were not sent by the government), the research being conducted, the future use of their responses and finally the researcher's lack of interest in their names and addresses. All that was done in Songhay, using the language style and gestures appropriate for the occasion. For instance, when approaching a female market goer for an interview, terms such as 'my sister', 'my mother' and the like tend to bring the researcher closer to the community. These strategies were coupled with the avoidance of hand shaking with female respondents that can quickly lead to cultural and religious shock.

The data quality control took place on the study site. But this work was preceded by a preliminary control immediately after the collection of the questionnaires and recording of interviews. Regarding the interviews, the researcher played back the recordings whenever these were available. It is worthy to note that seven laymen did not want their voices to be recorded; the same holds true with all first and second forms students whose voices were too low to be recorded, possibly because of their shyness. In any case, the researcher took all the answers on forms made available for the purpose.

A challenge that the researcher had to take up during the study was the expected number of pupils to interview in the two schools. In fact, when he went to interview the pupils, the researcher noticed that there were fewer pupils than expected: according to the headmaster, "*a big number of pupils have been withdrawn from the mother tongue-based schools and have joined private classical French-based schools. Every parent who can pay for the school fees of his child sends him to a private school*"[19]

The headmaster of Gaday A School explained that parents used to enroll their children in school without asking about the type of curriculum they would follow. But, when they are informed that their children are following a mother tongue-based curriculum, they will just go and withdraw them from the school and enroll them in a classical French-based school. But before they do so, they would go and tell the headmaster that they had sent their children to school to learn French and to become important people in life, not to learn Songhay, which they already speak.

This research is ethnographically oriented. "*Ethnography is the art and science of describing a group or culture*" (K. F. Punch, 2005, p.149). It aims at describing a culture and understanding a way of life. In the same sense, this study is investigating how groups of

---

[19] Information collected during informal talks with the headmaster of Faranjiray B School and confirmed in Gaday A School.

people such as headmasters, teachers, pupils, school partners, and laymen, etc. feel about and behave vis-à-vis mother tongue-based education. The researcher visited groups and interrogated the members on the issue.

This chapter has discussed the methodological procedures adopted in conducting the present study. It has specifically examined the descriptive approach adopted and the rationale behind it. It has also described the setting for the research which is the commune of Gao, a Songhay stronghold, presented the population for the study, made up of the people of the commune of Gao, and the sampling procedures adopted. That has been followed by the piloting phase meant to test the research tools, and the proper study to carry out. Finally, the chapter has described the research instruments used, namely the questionnaire and the structured interview, and their strengths and weaknesses, without losing sight of the underlying ethical issues.

Chapter two: Language and education in Mali: a historical overview

Education goes hand in hand with societal values and objectives. Where there are human beings, there is education, and education is carried out in language. But educational systems and the languages to carry them out vary according to societies. This chapter makes a chronological analysis of the three major periods of education and language use in Mali.

2.1. Language and pre-colonial education

This educational system is different from the modern one in that children, from birth to the age of six, stay with their mother, who takes care of them due to their physical and mental fragility. From that age up to around ten, there appears to be a gender distinction which takes the boy towards the world of man and the girl towards that of woman. The boy is initiated to the occupation of his father: collecting wood for cooking, keeping the cattle and farming. Another vital step in the education of the boy is circumcision, which prepares him for manhood and is celebrated according to the rites of each ethnic group. Ceremonies are organised and the boy is initiated into becoming a model citizen.

The girl on the other hand, is initiated to the domestic chores of her mother. She keeps her eyes on her younger brothers and sisters, learns family economy, cooking, goes to market, first, with her mother, then alone. Here again, and depending on ethnic groups, the girl undergoes excision which prepares her for womanhood.

All that traditional education takes place in the mother tongue.This way, both the boy and the girl acquire their mother tongue, in the full sense of acquisition, and learn some arithmetic, family economy, hygiene, respect of the elders, wisdom, and moral lessons in the world of tales, stories, and riddles around the fire.

The next stage introduces the child to social life. The leader of the group is chosen according to his physical and moral qualities, but that was done in accordance with the customs of the community. The rules of collective life, responsibility and solidarity are learnt, while games and wrestling ruled by loyalty and friendliness ensure physical training.

The initiation period puts some constraints onto the two groups, which have so far enjoyed some freedom meant to develop in them the sense of initiative and responsibility; this time, they are received, taken care of, and taught by the community's holders of wisdom, science and secrets:

> They learn the history of their society, the mysteries of life and death, the secrets of medicinal plants, the right period of cultivation and seeding. The young girl will learn about her duties and the obligations of a wife and a mother, she will learn about child diseases and how to cure them, etc. The young man will learn the rules of war and

hunting; he will be able to orient himself and understand seasons' mysteries, in short, all what will enable him to hold his responsibilities of man and future head of family (Mali, Ministère de l'Education Nationale, Contact Spécial, 1983, p.50)

The high significance of this type of education is that it is practical in the sense that learners can see the direct relevance and usefulness of their learning. It is linked to their own social, economic and cultural development; so they feel its significance in their future life as adults. In other words, teaching appears linked to practical life; at the same time the child's language competence (both linguistic and communicative) develops, giving rise to full mastery of the language spoken around the child. Elders play a key role in educating children. Was it not Hampaté Ba who said that in Africa *every old man who dies is a burning library?* A glance at some definitions provided by education specialists show that these people do not seem to go much beyond what traditional education used to teach. For instance, Buisson (1911) cited in R. Deldime and R. Demoulin (1975, p.45) conceives education as:

Action exerted by older generations on those who are not yet mature for social life. It aims at arousing and developing in the child a number of physical, intellectual and mental states which the entire political society and the social milieu for which he is particularly meant claims from him.

In plain words, education defined in these terms, prepares the younger generation to be effective in their future social life, and this is ensured by older people (in the family and the surrounding) and other people specially designated for the rest of the work.

R Deldime and R. Demoulin (1975, p.45) citing Lafon (1963) does not say more in his definition. Education is "*action exerted by an adult who has that responsibility, on a younger being for his physical, intellectual and moral development and his integration in the milieu for which he is meant*".

As to the German philosopher, E. Kant (1724-1804) cited in R Deldime and R. Demoulin (ibid), he points out that "*man is the only creature susceptible of education. By education, we mean the care (treatment, care) which his childhood demands, the discipline which makes him a man (in short), instruction with culture*". This last definition narrows down the concept of education to human beings, but still works in the same framework as the first two: the preparation of an immature person by a mature one for a future society.

There is a diversity of definitions provided and advocated, but they all seem to have four common features, that is at least the view held by René Hubert cited in R. Deldime and R. Demoulin:

1-Education is limited to mankind;

2-Education is an action exerted by an individual on another (or a generation on another);

3-Education is oriented towards an aim to achieve;

4-Education consists in acquiring behaviours which go with the natural bent of the individual.

These four characteristics can all be found in pre-colonial education. But traditional education tends to proudly transfer the same knowledge to different generations without evolution. Expressed in plain terms, traditional education does not seem to open opportunities for the learner to evolve compared to modern education: the same elements are taught and learnt and passed on to future generations without evolution whereas modern education is all the time evolving.

But pre-colonial education cannot all be narrowed down to just this system established by traditional education. Mali was one of the very few empires which enjoyed high prestige in education. In this sense, the cities of Timbuktu and Jenne in the 14th and 15th centuries in present day Mali constituted two world educational references (Mali, Ministère de l'Education Nationale, Programme Décennal de Développement de l'Education, 2000, p.4). Timbuktu was better known for its great university (Sankore University) where students and their professors met to teach and learn. That university received visitors from different parts of the world. Scholars in these two centres are believed to be at the same intellectual level as their Arab counterparts, or had even a higher level. History reports that Abderrahaman El Temini from Mecca (Saudi Arabia) was brought to Timbuktu (Mali) by King Kanku Musa, to teach at Sankore University. At his arrival, he found the level of education in that university so high that he felt obliged to go to Fez (Morocco) to study law before he came back. That university education was conducted in Arabic and was religiously oriented. It was conducted in a language which, in many cases, was not foreign to the users. In fact, there were and there still are so many native Arabs who live in the north of present day Mali, who are native speakers of the Hasaniya Arabic variety. This means that Arabic in Timbuktu and Jenne should not be perceived as foreign in comparison to colonial languages.

History equally demonstrates the existence of a Cameroonian hieroglyphic writing, the origin of which can be traced back to remote times, even though its development is rather recent. The Vaï syllabic writing system in Sierra Leone, and that of the Basa, have all been studied. Other writing systems include N'Ko in the Manding area, Tifinagh of Tuareg people in northern Mali, and the alphabetic writing of the Misibidi. These writing systems were used in the education of people.

It is true that these writing systems did have a large audience. African studies in pharmacy, mystic science, and the whole African philosophical thought, could have had a stronger impact on modern science if all that knowledge had been written. Nevertheless, Arabic, introduced with Islam, has served to preserve important elements of African science in spite of the attempt of colonisation to destroy the entire African history. And, as pointed out earlier, the language of education was always a local one. But whatever the language of education, the purpose was to train people for their future social life.

This first section has analysed the issue of language and education before the arrival and intrusion of the European colonisers in Africa. The next section will still focus on language and education, but in the colonial times.

2.2. Language and colonial education

The different elements analysed above are evidence that if colonisation had not intruded in the historical development of Africa, the continent would have had an intellectual level that would have challenged that of western education and its civilisation mission. There are three crucial questions the answers of which will give a better insight into colonial education: What was the mission of colonial education in French Sudan? How did that education look like? And, in what language was it carried out?

The questions are better answered by Brévié, the French West Africa General Governor:

The colonial duty and the political and economic requirements impose a double task to our work of education: on the one hand, the concern is to train indigenous executives who will become our assistants in all the fields, and to ensure the emergence of carefully chosen elite; on the other hand, the concern is to educate the masses as to bring them closer to us, and to transform their lives.... On the political ground, the concern is to make the natives know our efforts and intentions to tie them up to the French lifestyle. From the economic standpoint, the concern is to prepare the producers and consumers of tomorrow (Mali, Ministère de l'Education Nationale, Contact Spécial, 1983, p.52)

In other words, "*the aim of colonial education was to subdue people and to integrate them in the administrative system*"; and "*for that purpose, sons of chiefs are to be subdued and indoctrinated*" (Mali, UNESCO, 2004, p.5). And that was best achieved through the colonised people's mastery of the coloniser's language, French.

These views succinctly explain the colonial educational and language policy, basically centred on the training of indigenous assistants to serve and defend the sole colonial interests, the transformation of the lives of the natives to become mere followers of the coloniser, and the preparation of the future raw material producers and industrial product consumers. That makes a basic difference between the French colonial system (direct rule) and the British one (indirect rule). In fact, while the French colonisers proceeded with forced assimilation of colonised people, the British sought to preserve the language and the cultural identity of indigenous people.

The history of the Sudanese School can be traced back to the beginning of colonisation in French Sudan. The name, *French Sudan*, was given to the present republic of Mali in 1886. A year later, the first school, the *Hostage School* of Kayes was opened. The hostages were the sons of the conquered chiefs. The aim was the same as pointed out earlier to train future defenders of the French interests. Later on, other children would receive the same teaching, mainly in basic skills such as reading, writing, and some arithmetic.

In 1895, the the *Hostage School* became the *School of the Sons of the Native Chiefs*. On November, 24th 1903, General Governor Roumé signed the charter organising education.

2.2.1. Stages in the evolution of colonial education

Colonial education had three basic stages:

Stage one: 1903-1918:

This period set up the organisation of education. A decree signed in 1903 specified the objectives of education:

We need interpreters for the natives to understand us just as we need go-betweens belonging to the indigenous milieu by their origins and to the European milieu by their education, to make their people understand and to make them embrace this foreign civilisation for which they demonstrate an aversion difficult to defeat (Mali, Ministère de l'Education Nationale, Contact Spécial, 1983, p.3).

This system of acculturation placed the 'civilised' native in two positions: he is black, so he can never be close enough to the white coloniser; he is 'civilised,' so he does not want to be on equal footing with his native brother. Often he is rejected by either group. In this sense, an English professor of Sanskrit at Oxford University ironically observes:

I have met few men indeed educated, and a lot of men half-educated or ill-trained...They give up their own language, their own literature, their own religion, their own philosophy, and the rules of their own castes, the customs they've preserved for centuries, without however becoming good students in our sciences, sceptical honest people or sincere Christians (ibid, p.27).

The Swiss linguist, F. de Saussure (1898) worked in a different direction. He depicted the main idea behind colonial education and its cruel long term objective:

If the natives are reticent to the benefits of the civilisation we are bringing them, it's because their prejudices have not yet enabled them to understand the advantages they draw from it. These prejudices are preserved by the remains of their former states, their beliefs, their institutions and their languages. Let us suppress these remains of a remote past. If they are much rooted in the present generation, let's talk to future generations through education... Let's teach our language to the children, inculcate them our ideas and France will soon count by millions, otherwise new citizens, at least faithful and grateful subjects (F. De Saussure, 1898, in Mali, Ministère de l'Education Nationale, Contact Spécial, 1983, p.27).

Knowing the significant role of language in education, F. de Saussure proposes, inter alia, the suppression of the languages of the colonised people in education and their replacement by French, the ultimate long term aim being the total uprooting of these people. That is the reason why colonial education programmes exhibited the historical and cultural features of France, while those of the natives were either neglected or simply falsified. Learners ultimately came to learn more about France and little about their own land; this system aimed at making assimilation easier and quicker, preparing for the future *servants* of France.

Stage two: 1924-1945:

The period between the two world wars was characterised by a strengthening of the educational system. The end of the war and the victory of France over Germany led the former to strengthen its linkages with its colonies. Education became highly selective: first the children of the native chiefs, then those of the community leaders, followed by civil servants', soldiers', and finally the children of peasants. The local languages were banned from the classroom; only French could be used, reinforcing by the same token a policy of linguistic assimilation. And those who happened to speak their mother tongues were given a *token*, followed by punishment.

Different education levels came into being:

-Elementary School: it required four years of schooling;

-Regional School: it lasted six years at the end of which the candidate received the Indigenous Primary School Certificate;

- Evening Classes: they were organised for adult education;

-Higher Primary School: created in 1931, it lasted three to four years and led to administrative jobs. It also paved the way to the General Government School;

General Government School: there were seven such schools, three of which were in the French Sudan. They were:

-The Rural College of Katibougou that trained agricultural technicians;

-The Higher Technical School of Bamako that gave vocational training in specialised areas;

-The Veterinary School of Bamako that trained livestock specialists.

The four other schools were not located in French Sudan, but were shared by the different French West African colonies. They were:

-The William Ponty College for future teachers;

-The School of Medicine and Pharmacy of Dakar for medical doctors;

-The Rural College of Dabou (Cote d'Ivoire) for agricultural technicians or engineers;

-The Young Girls' College of Rufisque for future female teachers and midwives.

Stage three: 1948-1960:

That was the true period of acculturation and assimilation. The attempts of assimilation became stronger especially with the constitution of October 27th 1946 which stipulated that the colonies had become an integral part of the French Union, and later, part of the French Republic. This new status was to be acquired by the colonies themselves, and through true assimilation. In other terms, equality was acquired through the acculturation and assimilation of the natives. The period also witnessed the colonies demand of the end of the second-rate training in practice so far, and the call for new quality education equal to that of France. That situation gave rise to another re-organisation of the educational system in 1948 in French West Africa as presented below:

-*Primary School*: it required six years of training at the end of which the Primary School Certificate was delivered;

-*Secondary School*: some significant changes were observed:

The former *Higher Primary School* became *Lycée Terrasson de Fougères*, and new schools created: the *Collèges Modernes* of Bamako, Markala, and Diré trained teachers; the College of Katibougou became a secondary school, but continued to train primary school teachers.

-*Technical and Vocational Schools*: the former *Vocational School* became *Lycée Technique*, and the *Higher Technical School* became the *School of Public Works*.

-*Higher Education*: there was no higher education institution in French Sudan. French Sudanese had to go to William Ponty, University of Dakar, or to Abidjan to pursue their studies.

In fact, education was organised to serve the sole interests of France. Programme contents ignored specificities such as the language, culture and history of indigenous people.

There was no true African educational policy, nor language policy. For instance, philosophy classes taught the ideas of Socrates, Plato, Aristotle and the likes, while the African those of Amadou Hampaté Ba, Seydou Badian, Cheick Hamidou Kane, Birago Diop, etc, were ignored. Vocational and technical training rather intended for office workers instead of technical agents, as the training received was not adapted to the social and economic needs of the country. Bright students were sent to major and serve in education, and the rest had to either survive, or find employment in the public administration. The entire educational system suffered from this inadequacy between what the student learned and his or her future occupation. That is why it was frequent to see doctors, engineers, teachers, etc, who were obliged to be re-trained before they started their actual job. There was no continuity in programmes and classes. And the learner had to learn *all sciences of the world* at the same time, and the day of the exam, he had to make a synthesis of all that barrel of knowledge in order to answer the questions.

An important characteristic of the colonial educational and language policy was the exlusive use of French as the only medium of education, not even in association with any indigenous language. And as A. Kwaa (1996, p.1) points it out, the colonisers *"by their refusal to allow the use of indigenous languages as media of instruction even at the lower levels of primary education, they were teaching the students that their own languages were not good enough for their edification"*.

The result of such policy was mental enslavement for the wider majority of the population who did not know how to read write and compute. And only a handful of people could truly participate in matters of education, government, etc. It is as if France was using education to keep its colonies in a state of underdevelopment.

This brief historical presentation of the colonial educational and language policy does not aim at negating all what was done in terms of education in the colonial period. No one can deny that the colonial system trained many, if not, all of the leaders who drove their countries to political independence. But it also tried to assimilate the minds of the natives and attempted to negate their social and cultural heritage, especially their native tongues, and that, in favour of the assimilationist colonial language. So, the analysis rather intended to provide a comprehensive view of the conditions which gave birth to the Educational Reform of 1962, i.e., the emergence of a true Malian educational system.

2.3. Language and post-colonial education

Education specialists recognise three major periods in the education history of Mali:

-1960s: The period was characterised by reforms and a break from colonial education and language policy.

-1970s and 1980s: The period was characterised by international impulsion to gear education towards citizens' specific needs such as productivity, the native languages, the programme contents and the realities of the country.

-1990s: Experimentation of different innovations such as Education For All (EFA).

2.3.1 The period between 1960 and 1990

In fact, when French Sudan became independent in 1960, only 7% of its population could read and write (Programme Décennal de Développement de l'Education: Les Grandes Orientations de la Politique Educative, p.4). Furthermore, the newly independent country of 4, 300, 000 people had only 3 veterinarians, 8 medical doctors, 10 lawyers, 7 engineers, and 3 pharmacists (A.Touré, 1982, pp.190-1, cited in M. Canvin, 2003, p.144). The rest of the staff was French.

The educational system inherited from France could not meet the challenges of the social and economic development of the country. It should be remembered that colonial education only trained assistants for its own functioning. Newly independent Mali needed executives, not assistants, as there was no one to assist any more. The new educational authorities did not reject the entire colonial legacy. They rather reconsidered the whole system in light of the new educational objectives set, and therefore kept what was relevant, and improved or changed what was not.

2.3.2. The education Reform of 1962

The 1962 educational Reform can be defined as the set of changes which the educational system of newly independent Mali underwent, moving from colonial education, with its typically colonial educational aims, to a typically Malian educational system, with its own social and economic development aims. It brought huge changes aimed at meeting the urgent educational needs of the country after independence, and adapting education to the new context. The Reform affected all aspects of education in Mali.

The basic aims of the Reform of 1962 were to give:

-Both mass and quality education.

In 1962, the schooling rate was 12% (66,208 pupils); eleven years after the reform, this rate increased to 20% (229,879 pupils). Moreover, the curricula contents also saw innovations in terms of change or improvement. Additionally, family education, ignored in the colonial system (with all the negative consequences on the child future behaviour toward the community) came to be re-embraced due to its essential role in school education and in the child's overall education, particularly at a younger age (13-14), when s/he is very vulnerable. In short, the child was no longer taken out of the family circle; s/he was kept in this circle essential for his overall growth for the first nine years at school.

-Education which can train all the workers that the country needs for its various developement plans, and which saves the maximum of time and money.

Mali had just become politically independent. The country needed executives who could ensure its social and economic development; and that could only be done through a re-organisation of its educational system. Besides, the poverty of the country and the urgency of the needs required quality training saving both time and money.

-Education which guarantees a level allowing degree equivalences with the other modern states.

This appeared sound as the country was calling for quality education which could give the same level of competence as in the other nations.

-Education the content of which will rely, not only on the specifically African and Malian values, but also on the universal ones.

It was clear that Mali could not continue with colonial education which mainly taught the French and western culture to the French Sudanese. Education has, first of all, to rely on the values of the learner, and then the universal ones (for instance, the use of native languages as media of instruction).

-Education which decolonises the minds.

On the one hand, Mali wanted to educate its citizens to understand the colonial system which taught them that they did not have any past. On the other hand, it had to teach (or at least to remind) them their own values. That would include the linguistic dimension of that educational system with the use of the native languages as media of education.

The structure of the educational system became quite different from the French one, and involved the following levels:

-Basic Education and Literacy

At this level, one can notice the importance ascribed to the native values (including mother tongue-based literacy). Literacy has the advantge of training adults (but also young people) to read, write, and compute, and more importantly, to directly apply those skills to solve daily development problems in their milieu. At independence, only 2 % of adults could do so.

-Junior High School Teacher Training Colleges

As the country was engaged in mass and quality education, a large number of teachers were to be trained to carry out this educational task.

46

-Secondary, General, Technical, and Vocational Education

General and technical Education aimed at training executives, and Vocational Education, at training technical agents. It also prepared for higher education, which would train top executives.

-Higher Education.

This top level education was needed as the country had to train its own decision-makers capable of independent thinking on daily concerns. But, the focus of the reform was less on this level, and more on the first two, which constituted the cornerstone of any social and economic development.

The suppression of boarding schools (internship), the reduction of primary school to nine years instead of ten, the establishment of two exams (one in the sixth grade, and the other in the ninth grade), and the possibility of using the native languages in functional literacy programmes appeared as further important innovations in the new educational system.

Reforms had continued until the 1990s. In 1982, decree N° 159/PG-RM of July 19th 1982 encouraged (applied) linguistic research that should be conducive to the development of alphabets for many Malian languages. In parallel, a functional literacy policy was going on in Rural Development Operations such as the Malian Company for Textile Development.

2.3.3. The period between 1990 and 2002:

The advent of democracy in 1991 spured further significant changes. In this framework, law N° 99-046/ of December 28th 1999 gave a general orientation to education in Mali. That was followed in 2000 by a ten-year Education Development Programme which specified the different aspects of the Malian educational policy.

Today, and following the motto of former President, Alpha Oumar Konaré, *One Village, One School and/or a* CED[20] (Ministère de l'Education Nationale, 2000, p.7), almost each village in the country has its own school or CED or both; and nearly each Cercle has its own secondary school and academy.

This chapter has made a historical overview of language and education in Mali. The precolonial educational system was characterised by Islamic education which used Arabic, and Animist education which used native languages. As to the colonial educational system, it simply banned the use of local languages from school in order to alienate and assimilate indigenous people. The post-colonial system gradually re-introduced the local languages into

---

[20] Centre of Education for Development

education as the authorities came to be aware of the benefits of mother tongue-based education.

The choice of the language(s) (or even the dialect) of education in a multilingual community remains a big thorn in the flesh of language policy designers and planners. To better understand this difficulty, the next chapter will take a glance at the world linguistic situation, the linguistic landscape in sub-Saharan Africa and the distribution of the Malian languages with a special focus on Songhay and its dialectal varieties.

Chapter three: Linguistic diversity and language policy and planning

The world is a mosaic of visions and each vision is incarnated in a language. Whenever a language dies, a world vision disappears (David Crystal, cited in Rieks Smeets, 2006, pp.1-8).

Several studies have been carried out about the world's languages, but they have not been able to establish an exact number of languages, especially when the distinction between language and dialect is not clearly set, and research is still ongoing.

3.1. Linguistic diversity in the world

UNESCO recognises the existence of 6,700 languages in the world, 50% of which are endangered. Only 4% of the world population speaks more than 96% of these languages; more, 50% of these languages are used in only 8 countries including five from sub-Saharan Africa.

Other studies (cited in M. Canvin, 2003) have proposed different figures about the number of languages in the world. For Grimes (2000 CDROM) proposes a list of 6,809 living languages in 237 countries in the world. D. Crystal (1987, p.285) narrows this figure down to 4,500 languages. As to D. Nettle (1999, p.1), he comes closer to Grimes with 6,500 mutually unintelligible languages. The plain truth is that there is no agreement on the number of languages in the world (at times, even within the boundaries of the same country).

Linguistic diversity tends to be the rule around the world. Most countries are multilingual and only a few are monolingual. The table below presents the world's ten most linguistically diverse countries.

Table N°13: The ten most linguistically diverse countries in the world (table adapted from M. Canvin, 2003, p.14).

No.	Country	Population (million2000)	Number of languages
1	Papua New Guinea	4,800,000	823
2	Cameroon	14,900,000	282
3	Indonesia -Irian Jaya	1,600,000	263
4	United Republic of Tanzania	35,100,000	135
5	Chad	7,900,000	132
6	Indonesia -Maluku	1,500,000	128
7	Vanuatu	200,000	109
8	Solomon Islands	400,000	69
9	Central African Republic	3,700,000	69
10	Uganda	23,300,000	43
	Total	93,400,000	*2,053*

This table shows that 93,400,000 people in ten countries around the world speak 2,053 languages. Five out of ten of these countries are located in sub-Saharan Africa. The remaining five other countries are from Asia (Indonesia) and the Pacific (Papua New Guinea). However, the most linguistically diverse country in the world remains Papua New Guinea (in the Pacific) with 823 languages. The table below shows the distribution of the 6,809 world living languages.

Table N°14: Distribution of the world 6,809 living languages per region (table adapted from M. Canvin, 2003, p.7).

Region	Number of languages	Percentage
Africa	2058	30%
Americas	1013	15%
Asia	2197	33%
Europe	230	3%
Pacific	1311	19%

3.2. Linguistic diversity in Sub-Saharan Africa

The African continent is composed of fifty-two countries divided into two broad regions. The first of these regions is North Africa, very poor in languages (with only Arabic and Berber languages or dialects). No North African country is among the ten most linguistically diverse countries in Africa. The second is sub-Sharan Africa which is extremely rich in languages (2,058 languages).

Table N°15: The ten most linguistically diverse countries in sub-Saharan Africa (table adapted from M. Canvin, 2003, p.20).

No.	Country	Population (million2000)	Number of languages
1	Cameroon	14,900,000	282
2	United Republic of Tanzania	35.100.000	135
3	Chad	7,900,000	132
4	Democratic Republic of Congo	50,900,000	218
5	Côte d'Ivoire	16,000,000	77
6	Central African Republic	3,700,000	69
7	Benin	6,300,000	51
8	Uganda	23,300,000	43
9	Mozambique	18,300,000	39
10	Liberia	2,900,000	29
	Total	179,300,000	1,075

The table above shows that ten countries out of fifty-two have 179,300,000 inhabitants who speak 1,075 languages. That implies that Africa is one of the most linguistically diverse continents.

3.3. Linguistic diversity in Mali

Like most African countries, Mali has a population composed of different ethnic groups speaking different languages and dialects. The number of languages or dialects and their actual status are not always clearly established. While Grimes (2000 CDROM) in M. canvin (2003, p.136) counts forty living languages, SIL-Mali identifies thirty-six and Ethnologue (2005, pp.141-145) counts fifty. Most official language documents recognise thirteen written languages. Law N°96-049 of August 2nd 1996, pertaining to the modalities of the promotion of the national languages, recognises the following languages: Bamanankan, Bomu, Bozo, Dogoso, Fulfulde, Hassaniya, Mamara, Maninkakan, Soninke, Soŋoy, Syenara, Tamasheq, and Xaasongaxanŋo.

Mali is a multilingual country which needs an integrating multilingual policy. Such a policy should take into account the needs of the different language groups, the available resources, etc. That implies that for its language policy implementation, Mali will need to carry out research on its linguistic and sociolinguistic situation; that will help determine the languages to be used in formal education. Such research will equally help provide information on people's attitudes towards the languages they use. In addition, the knowledge internalised in the mother tongue (structure and use) will facilitate the learning of a second or a third language. In other words, the learning of another language should depart from the stock of knowledge already built in the first language.

The field of education has always been a threat to the authorities of the country because of the huge challenges it presents. One big challenge remains the choice of the learners' language of education in a highly multilingual country. French has long been used as the education medium for unifying purposes. And since the educational objectives aimed at have not been achieved, both language and education specialists have come to believe that the only tool for development and personal growth must come from the use people can make of their native languages in the education of their children. For that, research needs to be carried on those languages in terms of their number, the areas where they are used around the country, the number of speakers for each of them, the dominant ones in specific areas, and the scientific description of these languages for their subsequent use in formal education.

The language map of Mali

Given that the focus of this study is Songhay, the researcher will provide in the next section a glance at this language, its different dialects and the areas where they are used.

3.4. Songhay and its dialects

Songhay is a crossborder language shared by a number of West African countries, mainly Mali, Niger, Burkina Faso (in the area of Dori), and Benin (in the area of Dendi)[21]. Different names are used to identify the language. In Mali, the language is simply called Songhay; in Niger, it is called Zarma; in Benin, it is Dendi; and in Burkina Faso, it is Maranse.

---

[21] Mali, Ministère de l'Education de Base. DNAFLA and AEN. 1995. Guide de transcription et de lecture du Soŋay. Pp.4-5.

Songhay has been classified into different families. D Westerman (1927, 1952) found first that Songhay was a language isolate, but later, classified the African languages into families and put Songhay (like Mossi and Wolof) into the Sudanian family. M. Delafosse (1912), another linguist, divided the high Senegal-Niger languages into nine families and Songhay stood alone as a separate family. M. Delafosse (1914) later found that Songhay (just like Mande and Chadic languages) was an agglutinative language close to the Mande group. J. H. Greenberg (1963) definitely classified the language into the Nilo-Saharan family, after he had taken it out of the Niger valley language families and put it into the Chamitic-Semitic languages (like Berber, Somali, Arabic, and Hebrew). But P. F. Lacroix (1969) just rejected that new classification of Songhay. R. Nicolaï (1990) defended the Tuareg-Mande creole origin of Songhay. L. Bender (1995) and C. Ehret (2001) found Songhay to be Nilo-Saharan. Last, Nicolaï (2003) came back with the hypothesis that Songhay is the result of the evolution of a Hamito-semitic lingua franca. In short, the classification of Songhay still remains a problem despite several attempts to put it into a family. D. Crystal (2002, p.317) classified Songhay as a Nilo-Saharan language, but at the same time, recognises the unclear status of the Songhay group spoken by over 2 million people in an area between Mali and Nigeria.

Moving closer to the specific situation of Songhay in Mali, this language is essentially used in the regions of Gao, Menaka, Timbuktu and Mopti. Songhay has four main dialects: Gaawo senni (used in Gao), Tunbutu ciini (used in Timbuktu and Jenne), Hombori used in the area of Hombori, and Dawsak (a mixture of Songhay and Tamasheq) used in Menaka. Gaawo senni has been established as the standard form of Songhay used in formal education.

3.5. Linguistic diversity and language policy and planning in Mali: the state of the art

Language policy is defined as any decision taken by a State, a government or a commune meant for orientation in the use of one or more languages over an area or for regulation in use. R. B. Kaplan (1992, p.144) considers that:

A language problem occurs whenever there is linguistic discontinuity between segments of a population that are in contact. Such a discontinuity, of course, affects individuals as whole populations. A language policy recognises the existence of such discontinuity and proposes a principled solution to the discontinuity.

The history of the world is full of examples of language policies. The Israeli language policy helped elect Hebrew as official language (for use in government, administration, education, army, banking, etc) requiring new lexicon as the language was classical and liturgical. Another example is the Japanese language policy which permitted a controlled entry of foreign words in Japanese and a control of the way the new terms are written in the

53

language. A last example comes from the Philippines where some 250 languages exist, but the 1976 Constitution recognises a certain status for Filipino and English to be used for all official purposes; other languages such as Ilacano, and Cebuano are ascribed important status while a number of smaller languages are simply recognised as existing. The national language, Filipino-a fiction language which is an amalgam of the different languages of the Philippines-would emerge by itself. This policy of the Philippines could be an inspiring example for those Malians who would like to see all the citizens of the country use a common language. The thirteen official languages of Mali can be analysed and a single one will come out. That could help avoid possible tensions which could arise from a government decision to choose a single language. But sound criteria can also be used to select a single language: the degree of language rootedness, stability, standardisation, etc.

Language planning can be seen as the implementation of the proposed language policy. In the words of R. B. Kaplan cited in W. Grabe and R. Kaplan (eds.), (1992, p.144):

The language plan is the vehicle for implementing a language policy; it tries to solve the [language] problem by dealing with the individuals involved. In order to be effective, a language plan has to make it explicitly clear that adopting some other language behaviour than that already practiced brings some palpable benefit to the individuals involved.

On the one hand, it specifically aims at defining the functions or the status of the identified languages (Status Planning), i.e., *"selling new [or standardized] forms of a language to the language community"*. On the other hand,

It deals with such issues reaching standardization on questions of pronunciation, arriving at a means to represent the language orthographically, arriving at an agreement on standardization of spelling, morphology, and grammar, and preparing and disseminating dictionaries and pedagogic grammar (Corpus Planning) (ibid).

In Mali, status planning can be seen in the series of ordinances, decrees, etc., taken to value and promote the national languages as tools for the social, economic and cultural development of the country. For instance, the decrees of 1967 and 1982 and a law of 1996 confer the status of national language to thirteen languages. The 25th article of the 1992 constitution proposes the promotion and the officialization of the national languages. A further law of 1999 on education orientation gives the status of language of instruction to the national languages in the framework of functional bilingualism.

While corpus planning involves changing the shape of the language and draws heavily upon linguistic descriptions, status planning deals with changing the attitudes of the users of the language and appears rather political. D. Crystal (2002, p.366) believes that language planning implies the following four processes:

-norm selection: this involves the identification of one language or language variety (among very many) within a country for use for educational, official and other purposes.

-codification: in this case, there is a need to develop for the language an alphabet, a grammar, rules of spelling and pronunciation, and a set of norms for standard use if it did not have any.

-modernisation: science and technology bring new concepts; the language may have to take in loan-words, coinages using the native language roots.

-implementation: the chosen language or language variety (the standard form) will have to be officially implemented through its use at school as a medium of education, or for government publications, in the media.

In terms of corpus planning, all the Malian national languages studied so far have a basic lexis and a specialised lexis (national language versus French); only Fulfuldé and Bamanakan have a monolingual dictionary. Eleven languages possess a spelling-book and a calculation booklet. The systematic description of three languages, a brief description of four languages and a study on language dynamics in Mali have been conducted.

The implementation of the steps taken in both status and corpus planning are expressed in:

i)   Formal education: convergent pedagogy, and the new curriculum of basic education;

ii)   Non formal education: literacy and post-literacy centres of education for development, media, translation.

A special division of the former Ministry of Basic Education, the Abdoulaye Barry Language Institute (ILAB[22]), which later on became the Academy of Malian Language (AMALAN), implemented a five-year programme (2004-2008) meant to promote national languages. One basic aim of that programme was the planning of the languages. ILAB initiated a survey:

-to determine the boundaries of each language in each commune, cercle and region, and eventually the language atlas of the country;

-to assess the point of view of each commune about the choice of the language(s) of work (or national language), especially in multilingual areas. Seven hundred and two (702) communes out of seven hundred and three (703) were visited. Youwarou was the only commune not visited yet. The aim was for people to choose one or two languages in each

---

[22] Institut des Langues Abdoulaye Barry (Abdoulaye Barry Language Institute).

55

commune, circle or region which would be their language (s) of work. Questionnaires were distributed to people in the different communes of Mali. The work which began in 2003 was still going on and might take time because of the limited staff at ILAB. Regular missions were organised in the communes, and reports about the activities conducted were noted and presented to educational authorities. In the view of P. Guindo at ILAB, *"all the communes agree on the use of bilingual and even in few cases, trilingual education"[23]*. Communal organisations and local elects are arguing for the officialisation of the national languages, but the plain truth is that languages cannot be imposed upon people, and more importantly, communal elects face problems: on the one hand, they use the languages as media of work for their every day activities in their areas; on the other hand, once outside their communes, they are required to use French to guarantee mutual intelligibility. The policy of ILAB had been to proceed in such a way that the national languages become languages of work; but it is as if language planning is guiding policy-making in the present Malian context. The results of these field investigations would inspire the school authorities in the design of a sound policy.

P. Guindo equally believes that Mali should carry out careful work step by step in order to avoid the *"chaotic situation of Guinea in matter of language policy and planning"[24]*. What Mali is doing is the translation of specialised lexis, the development of monolingual dictionaries in each national language and the creation of terminology committees for the standardisation of dialects. That work would require both time and finances, while Guindo explains that *"donors are ready to fund everything except the national languages"[25]* because as the coloniser's motto goes, *"colonised people who lost their language are truly colonised, but colonised people who still keep on their language are only half colonised because they still keep their culture"* (Mali, Ministère de l'Education Nationale, Contact Spécial, p.71).

The programme also aimed at translating the official documents in the national languages, which have been chosen by the communes, so that the local elects could work in the languages of the people that they represent (education, justice, local administration, etc.). One thing which might appear strange is that bilingual education has been in place for more than ten years, yet only now is research on planning the national languages being conducted to determine the exact language areas in the 703 communes. But P. Guindo believes that the Ministry of Education has been at the forefront compared to the other ministries and services involved in the promotion of the national languages due for the most part to the emergency

---

[23] P. Guindo, personal interview: 04/04/2007
[24] Ibid.
[25] Ibid.

situation of the Malian educational system, i.e., the poor achievement of pupils which has prompted the school authorities to identify and propose immediate solutions, beginning with 'preliminary surveys'.

In sum, ILAB (which became later on AMALAN) has been working in partnership with the Malian Geographical Institute (MGI) to develop a language map of Mali. The significance of this map lies in the choice of the appropriate teacher for the appropriate language area.

A very important innovation in the new educational system remains the introduction of bilingual education with the aim of making the learner functional in all circumstances, and preparing him or her specifically for the economic development of the country, even if s/he were to drop out of school. This new system has been built on an analysis of the weaknesses and the serious limitations observed in French only-based education. The major aim of this bilingual education is to gear education toward development. It is only when the masses are educated (it does not matter in what national language, but the mother tongue remains the best medium) that true development can be ensured. This issue is detailed in the next chapter.

Chapter four: Impulsing mother tongue-based formal education

The interest of the Government of Mali in national languages as media of instruction can be traced back to the 1960's and 1970's, following a number of international conferences held on education. The first of these conferences was the UNESCO experts' meeting and its subsequent report publication in 1953; the second was the heads of states' Addis Ababa meeting of 1961; the third was the Accra intergovernmental meeting on cultural policies of 1975; and the fourth was the international seminar on the promotion of national languages and education in Africa held in 1976 in Lagos. All those conferences and several others were organised on how to improve the quality of education and facilitate access through the mother tongue.

It was only after the Second National Seminar on education held in 1978 in Bamako, that the true impetus was given to the use of native languages in education. At that time (i.e. in 1978), the concern of the Malian government was to study the different languages and the conditions for their use in education as soon as the means would allow. In fact, the government had understood that under-development stems from illiteracy: Mali became independent, and very few people could read and write; the vast majority of people were illiterate. So the task ascribed to the Ministry of National Education was to liquidate illiteracy and to study the native languages for their transcription.

Literacy can be done both in French and the local languages; but literacy in the mother tongue is far more cost-effective than literacy in another language like French; and what is more, mother tongue-based literacy does not prevent people from carrying out their daily activities. Additionally, people who become literate in their own languages will remain part of their communities, and will continue to effectively contribute in the development of their areas as the knowledge they hold is easily accessible to everybody. Thus, literacy helps people gain ready access to information about hygiene, agriculture, cattle breeding, economics, etc.

The government was convinced that development could not be achieved without functional literacy; therefore, functional literacy appears as an instrument to reduce the gap between literate and illiterate people, the means to enrich the cultural patrimony agonising with the disappearance of the elderly, the tool to absorb the remaining illiterate people, and the guarantee which endows a wider majority of people with the knowledge of their rights and duties as citizens. In short, it is an essential instrument to ensure sustainable local development.

4.1. The role of the National Directorate of Functional Literacy and Applied Linguistics

The government issued ordinance N°25/CMLN on July 2nd 1973, which created the National Institute of Functional Literacy and Applied Linguistics (INAFLA[26]) with three major objectives:

-To continue and strengthen adult literacy;

-To participate in the cultural promotion of the toiling masses through appropriate adult education forms having global and functional features;

-To study, on the basis of the acquired experience in this functional literacy, the possibility of introducing national languages in school education.

The creation of this institute and the objectives ascribed to it demonstrate, once more, the extent to which the officials of the first Republic were committed to fighting against poverty, and under-development; they also express the desire of those authorities to study and develop national languages and their use in formal education (either as subjects or medium of instruction).

Of course, the institute had gone through different phases before it appeared under the name of INAFLA: it was initially created in 1961 under the name of the National Literacy Centre (CNA[27]), with the primary purpose of promoting literacy in French. Then, in 1968 it became the National Functional Literacy Centre (CNAF) with the new aim of experimenting with a literacy programme, PEMA[28], in the local languages. In 1973, it became INAFLA, which was represented at the regional level by a Regional Directorate of Functional Literacy and Applied Linguistics (DRAFLA[29]). Two years later, on October 21st 1975, decree N°60/ CMLN changed the institute once more into a National Directorate for Functional Literacy and Applied Linguistics (DNAFLA[30]), represented at the regional level by a literacy section within the former Regional Education Directorate. Decree N° 159/PG-RM dated 19th July 1982 gave DNAFLA the role of language policy formulation. Four years later, the decree was ratified by law N°86-56/AN-RM of 24th July 1986.

Further changes took place and included law N° 00-048/P-RM of 26th October 2000, which created the National Directorate of Basic Education (DNEB[31]) with the aim of preparing and coordinating the formulated language policies; it was ratified by ordinance N°00-85 of 26th December 2000, and its reference terms were set by decree N° 00-0526/P-RM of 26th October 2000. Ordinance N° 01-044/P-RM 19th September 2001 created a new

---

[26] Institut National de l'Alphabétisation Fonctionnelle et de la Linguistique Appliquée.
[27] Centre National d'Alphabétisation
[28] Programme Experimental Mondial d'Alphabétisation.
[29] Direction Regionale de l'Alphabétisation Fonctionnelle et de la Linguistique Appliquée.
[30] Direction Nationale de l'Alphaétisation Fonctionnelle et de la Linguistique Appliquée.
[31] Direction Nationale de l'Education de Base.

language institute, the Abdoulaye Barry Language Institute (ILAB) and subsequent decree N°
01-516/P-RM of 22nd October 2001, set its terms of reference. DNAFLA finally became part
of the National Directorate of Basic Education, and the former role it fulfilled was given to
Centres of Education for Development (CED). The National Resource Centre for Non-Formal
Education (CNR-ENF)[32] was created to deal with the coordination of the education
programme, teacher training, and the production of didactic material for non-formal
education. ILAB continued research for the promotion of the national languages (MEN, 2004,
Programme Quinquennal de Promotion des Langues Nationales au Mali [2004-2008], ILAB,
p.7). It also initiated a five-year programme (2004-2008) to promote national languages. The
programme specified the objectives to reach for each year, the anticipated results, the
indicators of achievement, and the activities to be carried out. Its objectives were striking in
that they attempted to set up a design for the language planning of the 703 communes of Mali
by 2005, to comprehend the state of the art of research in the national languages, to develop a
linguistic atlas of the rural communes, and to propose a training programme for translators
and interpreters. The programme also included a six components action plan which indicated
the specific objectives to reach, the expected results, the indicators of achievement, the person
responsible for activities, the activities to be carried out, the cost, the partners involved, and
the periods of implementation.

-First Component: language planning design (both corpus and status planning);

-Second Component: promotion of translation and interpretation;

-Third Component: promotion of the learning of a second national language;

-Fourth Component: promotion of applied linguistic research;

-Fifth Component: application of New Technologies of Information and Communication
(NTICs) to national languages.

Further Changes took place with the Education Orientation Law and its Ten-year
Programme for Education Development (PRODEC) component, which specified the
constituents of basic education as follows: pre-school and special education, basic education
and non-formal education. The latter has two components: Centres of Education for
Development (CED) and Functional Literacy Centres (CAF).

4.2. Centres of Education for Development (CED)

Strategies to promote the use of the national languages in education have continued to be
implemented. It is in this framework that a seminar was held in 1999 in Bamako in order to

---

[32] Non-Formal Education National Resource Centre

study the domains and conditions of use of the native languages. The seminar recommended, among other things, the gradual generalisation of the use of the national languages in formal education (convergent pedagogy) to include even the 7th, 8th and 9th grades. The seminar further recommended the use of national languages in the civil service, decentralisation, justice and African integration (Mali, Ministère de l'Education Nationale, 25 août 1999, Rapport des Travaux de l'Atelier sur les Domaines et Modalités d'Utilisation des Langues Nationales, Pp.1-3).

A significant evolution in education is the creation of CEDs by the government with the aim of adapting education to the socio-economic realities of the country. Experimentation with CEDs was carried out between 1993 and 1997, within the framework of a Mali-UNICEF Cooperation Programme under the label YE-304-02 Non-Formal Education Project for non-schooled children and women and was piloted by DNAFLA with UNICEF financial support (Mali, Ministère de l'Education, PRODEC, 2002, Stratégie « un village –une école et/ou un CED », Guide pour l'implantation d'un Centre d'Education pour le Développement (CED), CNR-ENF, p.7). The CED strategy has been proposed as an alternative form of education for young people who actually need training but who cannot attend school for various reasons (there is a school but too far from the home, the child works with the family in the day, or is a school drop out, etc). CEDs are opened and managed by the community itself. As in Convergent Pedagogy, courses in CEDs are, in the first year, conducted in the learner's mother tongue. That is followed by the introduction of oral French in the second year, and written French in the third year. This first phase is theoretical with the teaching of disciplines in close connection with the learners' environment (health care, hygiene, agriculture, calculation, sanitation, etc). The fourth year, which is also the second phase, is practical: learner choose fields of interest to him to practice with the assistance of pedagogical advisors, teachers, service technical agents, etc.). Classes begin at 8:00 AM and end at noon, and are held five days a week and last for six months a year. There is flexibility in the organisation of classes as parents in some areas may need their children to carry out some domestic chores (S. Kane, M. Keita and S. Sarr, 1999, Pp.1-12). The CED policy as advocated by the government aimed at achieving universal schooling: to give a chance to every child to have at least minimum education.

A basic advantage of the CED policy is that pupils become literate, learn about their environment and put what they have learnt into practice. More, all of that learning takes place in their own community, without affecting very much their daily activities. That ensures their personal development and that of their own social milieu.

4.3. Functional Literacy Centres (CAF[33])

A literacy policy should not have the sole aim to teach individuals how to read and write, but should also tend towards creating literate societies where everyone can use his literacy to search for liberty, new opportunities, and personal growth, and where literacy contributes to economic and social development (UNESCO, 2006, Rapport Mondial sur l'EPT, p.229)..

CAFs are training centres created to fight against illiteracy in the country and are strategically placed around rural development areas such as *CMDT, Opération Riz Ségou,* etc. They consist of one of three forms: female-only, male-only, or mixed centres according to the socio-cultural views of the community which hosts them.

At the first stage (literacy), the centres aim to train adults to read, write and compute in their mother tongues; and

At the second stage (post-literacy), they aim at gearing that knowledge to the social and economic development of their environment. While classes of stage one relate to how to read, write and compute, those of the second pertain to agriculture, cattle breeding, health, etc. and are attended by those declared neo-literate after a test (i.e., making their learning functional).

CAFs have undergone a long history. As pointed out earlier, it all started with the creation of CNA in 1961 to address illiteracy; in 1968, CNA turned into CNAF[34] to deal with the World Experimental Literacy Programme (PEMA); in 1973, CNAF was replaced by INAFLA, which, in 1975, in turn became DNAFLA.

There have been three programmes to achieve the set literacy objectives:

The National Programme: That consists of a set of sub-programmes to lower illiteracy rates in Mali and involves:

1961-67: the liquidation of illiteracy in ten years (literacy in French);

1967-72: PEMA or functional literacy;

1975-79: an ACDI programme meant for the improvement of productivity and the quality of life of cotton and cereal farmers, and for the acquisition of the reading skill;

1977-92: FNUAP projects (using cameras) for women's education, awareness-raising and information;

Third World Bank Project or mass (functional) literacy;

EO27 Project: women and the young girls' literacy.

The Sectorial Programme: the literacy component of the Rural Development Operations.

---

[33] Centre d'Alphabétisation Fonctionnelle (Functional Literacy Centre).
[34] Centre National d'Alphabétisation Fonctionnelle (National Functional Literacy Centre)

NGO Programmes: programmes conceived and implemented by NGOs and organisations at the grassroot level.

CAFs are still fighting against illiteracy in the different villages around the country; their use shows once more the desire of the government to involve everybody in the development of the country.

4.4. The World Bank's support to mother-tongue-based education

The World Bank has been increasingly intervening in the education sector, mainly in basic education. The aim has been to improve the functioning of the Malian educational system (public and community schools, including convergent pedagogy schools). The World Bank worked in the framework of the strategic choices of PRODEC and therefore encouraged the use of the national languages (and French) in formal education. By the same token, it put emphasis on adult literacy in order to ensure greater and more effective community involvement in school management. In 2002, the Learning Support and Improvement Project in basic education, one of the projects funded by the World Bank, trained 3,775 teachers, recruited and trained 1,854 contractual teachers in convergent pedagogy, edited 161,000 copies of books for reading-writing in Bamanakan, Fulfuldé, Songhay, Tamasheq, Dogoso and Soninké, and printed 33,000 copies of books in six languages. The Bank also funded the Professional Training Consolidation Project, and worked hand in hand with PRODEC to increase the schooling rate to 95 % by 2010 (Banque Mondiale, Partenariat Mali/Banque Mondiale, 1999/2000, Bureau de la Banque Mondiale au Mali, Pp-27-32).

4.5. The role of the African Language Academy (ACALAN)

The Mission for the African Language Academy (MACALAN) was created by decree N° 00-630/PRM of December 19th 2000 (E. Sagara, and S. Diakité, 2002, p.5). The aim was to pave the ground for the opening of an African Language Academy (ACALAN) in relation with the OAU General Secretariat. Right after its creation, the mission started meeting organisations and ministries responsible for education.

In fact, since independence (usually around the 1960's for most states), several attempts have been made by African states to develop policies on the study and use of their native languages. Thus, the 29th Article of the OAU Charter of 1963 stipulates that the languages of work of the organisation were, if possible, the African languages and English, French, Arabic and Portuguese (M. Diouf, 2002, Pp7-8). That was further strengthened, six years later, by the 1969 Algiers' Pan African Cultural Manifesto, which called for the promotion of African languages through their use in education and in the translation of important scientific works of humanity. The 1975 Accra (Ghana) Intergovernmental

Conference Final Report on Cultural Policies in Africa (UNESCO-OAU) appears as the basis of post-colonial African cultural (and to a lesser extent) language policies. Its recommendations led to the creation of various regional centres.

In July 1976 in Port Louis (Mauritius), OAU adopted the African Cultural Charter, a combination of the Cultural Charter project of the African Cultural Institute and the Algiers' Cultural Manifesto. It also resulted in the emergence of regional centres but did not lead to a true use of African languages by governments. By 1980, the Lagos Action Plan for the Economic Development of Africa made no reference to African languages.

The results of the 1986 first conference of OAU African Ministers of Culture (Port Louis, Mauritius) produced two significant documents, all of which ascribing a salient role to African languages. The first document, the African Language Action Plan, was developed by the Inter African Language Bureau (Kampala, Uganda). The second document named Kiswahili as an OAU language of work. The resolutions of the conference were ratified by governments, but no further step took place.

The 1991 Abuja (Nigeria) Treaty creating the African Economic Community took a step backward and eliminated African languages from its scope, while the 1993 Regional Plan of Oral Tradition Collection in Southern Africa (Hararé, Zimbabwé) made recommendations which, unfortunately, have never been implemented. The 1997 Intergovernmental Conference on African Language Policies (UNESCO-OAU-ACCT) made decisions about African languages, but have never been implemented, especially at the level of use of these languages by African Intergovernmental Organisations. The Language Division at UNESCO was even closed. The 1999 Action Programme of the Education Decade (Hararé, Zimbabwé) encouraged the use of African languages in education. Unfortunately, little change was noted in the language habits of African organisations and countries. The 2000 African Union Treaty (Lomé, Togo) took a step forward and proposed the use of African languages as OAU languages of work, but arriving at the same proclamation made by OAU in 1963, 37 years earlier.

The failure of these African organisations to promote African languages, in terms of research and use at the state and continent levels, led the Malian government to create in 2002 a Pan African organisation, the African Language Academy. One of the main objectives of the Academy is to identify the reason why African languages are not used in African intergovernmental organisations and to propose solutions to this problem.

4.6. A further step: the NEF[35] policy

The idea of the NEF policy came out in 1994 after an analysis of the problems that the Malian educational system was facing, namely, the multiplicity of educational experiments, the low involvement of the grassroot communities, the high rate of school drop-outs, etc. The NEF policy relies on three major principles:

-i) cultural identity (the national languages);

-ii) gearing school to life;

-iii) and the involvement of all the actors in school life.

Like Convergent Pedagogy and the later Curriculum, the NEF policy heavily relies on the native languages as media of education since the classical French-based school system has proved to be ineffective. Therefore, the new policy aimed at promoting the national languages, and the cultural values associated with them, through their integration in the learning process of the child. Advocates for the NEF policy ascertain that the child develops his very first thoughts and makes his/her first contact with the social milieu in the mother tongue. Any attempts to prevent him/her from using that language are tantamount to preventing him/her from thinking. The rationale behind NEF is that to develop the African educational systems, it is necessary to promote these national languages by ascribing them an official status and a full pedagogical role beside the second language. In plain words, the proponents of the policy consider that both the mother tongue and the second language would be concomitantly used with the purpose of developing functional bilingualism in the learner. It is good to remember that the NEF policy came into being when Convergent Pedagogy in experimentation since 1979, had already started its generalisation in the Malian public schools. The NEF policy however, failed because of lack of support from teachers' unions and community involvement.

This chapter has overviewed the use of native languages at both the continent and state levels. It has highlighted the desire of African governments to carry out research in their languages for their future use as media of international communication in order to achieve African linguistic independence. It has further demonstrated that there have been both national and continental attempts at developing effective language and education policies.

At the national level, the different changes that have been observed in the Malian educational system and the alternative educational forms and languages policies which have been proposed express the conviction of the Malian authorities that development cannot be ensured

---

[35] Nouvelle Ecole Fondamentale (New Primary School).

65

without at least, literacy. The changes equally demonstrate the willingness of the government to educate the citizens for the development of the country, putting emphasis on mother tongue-based instruction. In this sense, the Ministry of National Education is trying to kill two birds with a stone, combining in primary school education, both French and the national languages, while also paying attention to literacy.

Chapter five: Convergent pedagogy: an overview

It appears as a teaching methodology based on the assumption that learning departs from the strategies the learner has developed in the acquisition process of the mother tongue and the gradual transfer of those strategies to the learning of another language. Convergent Pedagogy has the following characteristics: it is a method of learning, a differentiated method, a method of projects and a language method.

5.1. A method of learning

Learning proceeds through hypothesis formation about what to learn, the trial of the formed hypothesis, its adoption if it works, its alteration if it fails, and the development and trial of a new one. J. Piaget (cited in R. M. Beard, 1972, pp.2-5) uses the terms *accommodation, assimilation and adaptation* to describe the processes of learning in which the infant is involved. In this sense, learning is perceived as a process of constant transformation and adaptation of the developed skills to new environments. In the words of M.Wambach (1995, p.9):

The child should be allowed to autonomously find out his way to knowledge by giving him a maximum of help, by opening for him multiple ways in order to arouse all his potentials, to value all his personality resources and to increase his creativity power.

Indeed, what makes sense to the child and what he can learn from is what he experiences. Thus, the center of the learning process remains the learner himself.

Convergent Pedagogy is centred on the learner, his real-life experience, and his environment. The method considers that the trainers are different and so are the trainees. Children grow up in their families, which give them each a form of education that they bring to school. The least that can be done is to take into account what the infants have received in the family if they are really to make sense of their school training. To ignore this aspect could be tantamount to exposing the children to contents which would make no sense to them. This is why great importance should be given to the mother tongue, susceptible of guiding the pupils through all types of learning.

5.2. A differentiated method

M. Wambach (1997, p.19) conceives a differentiated method as "*one which aims to set up a number of diversified learning types in order to enable heterogeneous level learners to reach the same goals using different paths*". This looks all the more true that teachers have different personality types, and make use of different teaching methods. Likewise, pupils are different and usually come from different families with different education and different social backgrounds. But whatever the differences, they contribute to enrich their learning.

5.3. A method of projects

The term *project* is used to refer to motivation for teaching, a means to apply and induce knowledge. The role of school is to develop the child's intellectual capacity. The child is taught to become a future social being, but that, with regard to his social context. In plain words, the project is a functional task the pupil is to carry out, and which he finds motivating and which causes learning to take place. Therefore, *"to recognise that writing and the appending learning activities are social brings teachers to put their strategies in the framework of projects"* (ibid. p.20).

5.4. A methodology of languages

Convergent Pedagogy is a method of oral expression that includes bodily and musical expression, language immersion and activities to liberate speech, the comprehension of oral language, role-play, grammar and oral discourse. Bodily and musical expression involves breathing and musical exercises that are used for relaxation, but also for contribution in the development of intelligence as the infant comes to discover his own breath and that of people surrounding him, and as he comes to take these people into account in breathing. Besides, they contribute to the development of abstract thoughts, mental images, multi-sensory arousal, creativity, and serve to unite the mind and the body. The result is relief, relaxation, and freedom from inhibition in speech. That feeling of well-being generates a greater openness to external stimuli. Hence:

> *The music strikes deep the psyche of the individual, creates the aptitude for communication, increases internal quietness, and fosters the re-establishment of basic rhythms.*
>
> *When the body expresses itself in perfect harmony with the music, can't we say that they form a whole, in perfect harmony?* (ibid).

A significant role played by mental images in particular is that they ensure understanding, memorisation, but more significantly, novel associations, the basis for all learning activities. Similarly, the practice of bodily and musical exercises is conducive to the creation of a group which ensures the blossoming of the members and ensures a healthy learning climate. On the other hand, multi-sensory stimulations relate to attention to body postures such as relaxation or tension, openness attitude, etc., and the level of breathing. That is why learners with concentration problems experience accelerated breathing rates, and high muscular tension. And that is why deep breathing, a slow heart rate, and relaxed muscles are used as strategies to ensure healthy learning conditions. M. Wambach (1997, p.26) citing R. Muccielli, (1974) thinks that the body image, that is, *"the balanced resolution of a conflicting relation between the physical self and the external world,"* gradually develops thanks to bodily and musical exercises.

Likewise, phonetic rhythms are practiced to develop, in the learner, awareness about the connection between the body and speech. There is an association between breathing, the body movements and the piece of music being listened to, in the indicated language. That appears all the more significant that the acquisition of rhythm, intonation, the different types of sounds and the production of sentences should be in harmony with the music being played. Language immersion and relaxation activities are centred on the story which appears as the central element in the implementation of this method and is present in all the pedagogical units of both languages from the first to the sixth grade. Language immersion also involves exposing learners to rich, varied, affectionate, and authentic language in functional situations (e.g., the speech and explanations of the teacher, etc.). Stories have the psychoanalytic aim of striking deep at the sub-consciousness of the infant and of teaching him about what life is made up of. The language immersion activities taking place simultaneously with the bodily and musical exercises have a very deep relaxation effect. They also help develop, among other things, creativity, imagination (the teacher partially tells a story and the pupils terminate it), and oral expression (the learners make a verbal role-play of the story the teacher told them) (Mali, Ministère de l'Education Nationale, 2001).

Stories also possess a salient linguistic feature as M. Wambach (1997, pp.29-30) citing G. Rodari (1979) points out:

We could never know the very moment when the child listening to a story assimilates by impregnation, relations between the elements of discourse, discovers the use of a modal, the function of a preposition; but I am almost certain that the story represents for him an abundant collect of information on the language. The intense mental activity he allows to understand the story, is partially used to comprehend the words which make it, to establish analogies between them, to make deductions, to widen or narrow down, to specify or correct the field of a signifier, the boundaries of a synonym, the sphere of influence of an adjective.

That way, the child becomes familiar with the text structure on the basis of which the writing skill is developed.

Around the end of the child's first year of learning a second language, familiarisation with writing takes place when he is asked to find out words from a book which contains the story he read or listened to, and to complete or modify that story, or to think about a new passage that he will tell his classmates.

In terms of narration, children sit and listen to the teacher who tells or helps them listen to the story in the mother tongue. In telling the story, the teacher pays attention to rhythms, intonation contours, pauses, gestures, look, and voice. That ensures careful listening and also alternation between tension (when learners are listening) and relaxation (when the teacher pauses for learners to internalise).

M. Wambach (1997, pp.31-32) proposes different strategies to exploit stories in the classroom. A first technique consists in the teacher telling the story, pausing somewhere, asking the pupils to imagine the rest, and then telling the end. That frees the learners from inhibition, drives them to talk, to anticipate, and to discover and learn the structure of the story. A second strategy could be for the teacher to tell or read the story, and ask the pupils to role-play it. A third technique would be for a pupil to read or listen to a cassette recording then explain the content to his or her classmates. A fourth strategy can be for a group of pupils to read a passage or listen to a recording about it, then role-play it to their class or to another class. A fifth technique consists in the teacher telling an illustrated story to the class. At the end, the pupils are asked to arrange the pictures in the correct order. A last strategy may be to ask pupils to build a story on the basis of illustrations which they put in the right order. Later, they tell or write about it and present it to their classmates.

Understanding oral language is crucial in carrying out these activities. Therefore, all the activities of audio-recordings, role-play, readings, story telling, etc. aim to contribute to oral language comprehension. Other activities can be based on radio broadcasts, interviews, conferences, and debates.

The learners build up meaning on the basis of some knowledge about communication situations. Such knowledge pertains to the identity of the speaker/listener, the reason, place and time of the conversation. From that, pupils form hypotheses about the content of the message. The hypotheses are either confirmed (in this case, the expected information integrates what was internalised) or refuted (in which case the learners develop new hypotheses).

The development of the ability to comprehend oral language relies on the acquisition of behaviour types such as self-confidence, intuition, imagination, prediction and sensitivity to rhythms and intonation patterns in the different exercises in the mother tongue, but more importantly within the framework of a project. That is why authentic materials are highly recommended.

There is usually a methodological procedure in the exploitation of materials for oral expression comprehension:

- Before the learners listen to a tape or read a passage, the teacher prepares them for the activity and announces the information to listen for. For instance, if the topic is about malaria, the teacher can say: last time we talked about infectious diseases. Today, we are going to listen to a doctor giving advice about how to avoid malaria and how to cure it once a person has caught it.

-After the pupils have listened or read the message, the teacher asks some questions to check their level of understanding. It may happen that the pupils, depending on the nature of the activity, ask questions to each other (in the case of a project) to collect specific information for their tasks.

Role-play activities and their significance in the liberation and personality development of learners have already been noted. When pupils role-play an activity, they put themselves in the place of a person and act as that person would, but at the same time, they tell about who they are, or at least who they think they are. According to M.Wambach (1997, p.45) citing A. Schutzenberger (1981):

The role-play activity allows people to do as if they were in the reality: they live in daily situations and problematic situations in a small group in total security. By (dint of) playing different real or fictional roles they come to discover themselves, feel themselves as they are and as they appear in the eyes of the others.

A learner's choice of a role to play is always guided by some internal drive. Role-play activities begin as early as the first classes in the language (first or second). They are usually inspired from stories, authentic materials, and dialogues.

When the activity is inspired from a story, pupils listen to or read the story. The teacher then asks them to choose roles and play them. They select the space and time for them, and begin the play. The story can also be played to another group. Of course, the actors are explained the appropriate gestures, body movements, pronunciation, and mimicry. The same applies when the activity is inspired from a dialogue. Usually, there is a general framework developed, and on the basis of that learners improvise a text. Pictures can be used as part of role-play activities to illustrate dialogues. However, before that, pupils should be taught to read them.

Role-play can be non-/verbal. Non-verbal role-play uses gestures, body movements, and mimicry and is generally recommended for a beginning activity in a second language; it gradually becomes verbal when the learners develop the ability to add or combine words and phrases. When it is verbal, the teacher presents the pictures, plays the dialogue, and makes the characters speak with the different intonation patterns, rhythms, etc; after the second play, the teacher asks the learners to develop a role-play about the activity.

Developing awareness about grammar remains an essential element in conducting the activities. Grammar can be seen as the sum of formal knowledge (phonetics, phonology, morphology, syntax, semantics) that a person has about a language, the formal rules governing language use. Most language learners equate grammar to morphology and syntax (comparable to N. Chomsky's 1957 *linguistic competence*). But, whatever it is and however it is perceived, grammar knowledge ensures correct formal language production. Every speaker of every language (save for abnormal people) necessarily knows and uses the grammar of that language.

In the context of Convergent Pedagogy, awareness about grammar is made in both oral (in the study of language functions and notions in the oral discourse) and written activities (grammar extracted from written passages). Pupils are taught the use of both language functions and notions in oral exercises through role-play, dialogues, language immersion, etc. Writing activities involve the production of texts, language functions and notions and speech acts. Various functions and notions with various meanings are expressed by speech acts according to contexts of use and intonation patterns. Teachers should pay particular attention to this aspect of a language.

The methodology does not lose sight of discourse construction. Pupils and teachers construct and use discourse all the time. Teachers tell stories to their pupils who, in their turn, re-tell the heard stories to their classmates and thereby construct discourse. Therefore, pupils should be introduced to discourse right from the beginning of learning by exposing them to the language (listening to stories); but it is better if this can be done within the framework of a project where the learner will have to defend his point of view and where listeners will have to anticipate and to adapt to unexpected situations.

Learners also need to be introduced to written discourse through the use of scrapbooks or class memory, i. e., the teacher writes words, phrases and texts (notices, instructions, etc.) and posts them up on the walls of the classroom. The development of written discourse usually depends on the level acquired by the learner in oral discourse.

Scrapbooks remain the basis for writing activities and the more diverse they are the more rapidly the pupils will learn to read and write. Functional writing is developed through exercises of text reconstruction, class memory, and other related activities drawn from dictation. It can also be done within the framework of project-based education.

Creative writing is introduced when the learner is exposed to stories with emotional constructs, to painting, movies or music. Inspired, the child is then asked to write about his own feelings. Feelings may also relate to other emotional situations such as love or death.

In the development of the reading skill, it is discovery-reading, also called sight-reading which is used. For instance, the learner comes with a piece of authentic writing in the mother tongue the meaning of which he longs to discover. The teacher helps him understand the passage. Passages may equally be proposed by the teacher especially when the student is unable to do so. They should be clearly written and posted up on the blackboard and in such a way that they can easily be hidden and uncovered whenever necessary. In fact, one discrete role of the teacher is to raise the learner's curiosity by uncovering the text at a particular time for the pupils to quickly screen it and by hiding it at a specific period to allow them to make sense of their readings (meaning and structure) through the development of hypotheses. Usually after a semester spent on doing such activities, part of the class becomes independent. A glance at language use under Convergent Pedagogy indicates that the two languages involved (French and the mother tongue) are distributed as presented in the table below.

Table N°16: Distribution of Bamanankan and French in the experimental schools of Ségou (adapted from Y. Haidara, 1998, p.26).

%	1st grade	2nd grade	3rd grade	4th grade	5th grade	6th grade
25%			Mother tongue	Mother tongue	Mother tongue	Mother tongue
50%	Mother tongue	Mother tongue				
75%			French	French		
100%		French			French	French

This section has examined the theory and practice of Convergent Pedagogy as developed by M. Wambach. The aim was to provide the reader with insights about the methodology. The next section presents the steps in the introduction process of the approach in the Malian educational system and the subsequent legal framework.

5.5. Convergent Pedagogy: steps and legal framework

As pointed out in the introduction of this work, the desire of the government of Mali to use the native languages as media of instruction with the aim of improving the quality of education can be traced back to independence. In fact, two years after independence, decree N° 235/PG-RM of October 4th 1962 indicated in its fourth article that education was carried out in French before the country had the means to conduct it in the native languages. The decree demonstrates by the same token the awareness of the government of the important role that local languages could play in the education of the masses. It should be remembered that at independence, 93% of the population could not read and write. With such a high rate of illiteracy, development was not possible.

Two years after that important step, the first seminar on education was held. It took place from December 28-29, 1964 and proposed to use the native languages to teach people how to read and write as soon as the conditions would allow. Three years later, in 1967, decree N° 85/PG-RM set the alphabet and the grammar for four languages (Bamanakan, Songhay, Fulfulde and Tamasheq). In the same process, the conference of executives held from December 5- 9, 1968 proposed, among other things, to put into effect children's right to education. Decree N° 57/PG-RM of April 20th 1970 strengthened the previous one, and went further by indicating that education was to be conducted in French, and the national languages whenever possible. The second national seminar held on December 18-24, 1978 finally made the decision of introducing local languages into the educational system at the elementary level. DNAFLA was in charge of examining the possibilities of using the languages in the educational system. The service continued to play a significant role in both functional literacy and the study and use of the national languages in formal education (Y. Mariko, 1993, pp.8-9). The first article of decree N° 159/PG-RM of July 19th, 1982 officially recognised ten languages as national (Bamanakan, Bomu, Bozo, Dogoso, Fulfuldé, Mamara Sénoufo, Syenara Sénoufo, Soninke, Songhay, and Tamasheq) and established alphabets for each. By the same token, the decree encouraged further linguistic investigations in the remaining languages.

Further changes took place with some constitutional amendments. For instance, the 2nd article of the Constitution of the Republic of Mali (1992) recognises freedom and equality in rights and duties of all citizens and bans segregation in all its aspects including language. Furthermore, the 25th article of the same Constitution recognises French as the official language of the country and stipulates that law will determine the status of the national languages and the conditions for their promotion.

The addition of three more languages to the list, (namely Hasanya, Maninkakan, and Xaasongaxanŋo) was made by law 96-049 August 23rd, 1996. A last element in that process was the 10th article of law 99-046 of December 28th, 1999 which provides that education will be conducted in French and in national languages. It also states that the conditions of use of these languages will be set by an ordinance of the ministers in charge of education.

In very practical terms, the failure at all levels of the traditional classical French-based teaching methodology, the success of functional literacy, the conviction that mass education is only possible in the national languages and is conducive to true development, the desire to promote and re-value the native languages and their culture, and to educate the maximum of citizens, led the authorities of DNAFLA to undertake two missions in Segu and Koolikoro. Their aim was to open experimental classes in Bamanakan, but in areas where classical schools did not exist, but where there were literacy centres. That was to avoid creating conflicts between people of the two types of education. The missions were to prepare the ground for experimentation with the use of information and awareness-raising of people, the building of classrooms, the enrolment of pupils and the buying of school supplies. That first experimentation was followed by a second one in 1987 with four national languages in concommittant use with French.

Following the positive results of experimentation in these two regions, the Ministry of Basic Education decided in 1994 to expand the methodology (both in terms of the number of languages and the areas and schools concerned). Regarding the languages, eleven were introduced in bilingual education, namely, Bamanankan, Fulfuldé and Songhay (1994), Tamasheq, Dogon and Soninké (1995), Bomu and Syenara (1998), Bozo and Mamara (2000) and Khassonké (2001) (Y. Haidara, 2005, p.32). Further research was needed in the two other national languages (Hasaniya and Maninkakan) in order to introduce them in education.

Research continued in order to determine the effectiveness of the methodology. Thus, a study by M. M. Konaté and P. Tamboura (1999, p.18) compares the results in mathematics and French of the 7th grade entrance exam of Classical and Convergent Pedagogy schools. The study concludes with the following figures: Convergent Pedagogy: 73% of rate of success; Classical School: 14%.

Table N°17: Success rate per year of the students of the two types of school in Mathematics and French.

Year of evaluation	Success rate in Convergent Pedagogy schools		Success rate in classical French-based schools	
	Mathematics	French	Mathematics	French
		51.2		49.5
1997		56.0		52.9
1998	52.8	48.7	35.7	39.5
1999	57.6	48.4	40.0	45.2

The results in the table above clearly show that bilingual pupils perform higher in mathematics and French than the monolingual ones for the three years studied. The same holds true with vocabulary, comprehension, arithmetic, measurement, and geometry. In grammar and conjugation however, monolinguals perform slightly better than the bilinguals counterparts (Y. Haidara, 2005, p.33). These results are supported by those of the diagram below which compares the success rate per region of the pupils of the two types of school:

Table N°18: Success rate per region of the pupils of the two types of school on the 7th grade entrance exam of 2000.

Regional Education Directorate	Convergent Pedagogy school pupils' success rate	Classical French-based school pupils' success rate
Kayes	68.10	49.04
Koulikoro	92.90	61.00
Sikasso	65.10	46.03
Ségou	46.69	45.12
Mopti	79.22	51.03
Timbuktu	62.00	62.01
Gao	59.56	53.51
Bamako	75.54	56.75
National %	68.57	52.34

The diagram shows that, except for the region of Timbuktu, where monolingual schools perform slightly higher than the bilingual ones (with a difference of 0.01 %), the success rate in bilingual schools is higher in all other regions of Mali. As to the special case of Timbuktu, it may be that people in that region have a greater openness to French due to the large number of tourist attractions. Again, this tendency is reinforced by another table (below) which presents the results of a comparative study between the two types of schools from 1994 to 2000. The success rate in bilingual schools is higher than that of the classical ones in all the periods indicated except for the year 1995 where the latter perform higher.

It is also striking that Ségou which scored 73.91 % (M. Wavelellah, 2002,p.25) of success rate in 1993 in experimentation, was also the only region to have scored very low in 2000 for both bilingual and monolingual schools (respectively, 46.69 % and 45.12 %). The table below gives a better illustration.

Table N°19: Success rate per year of the pupils of the two types of school on the 7th grade entrance exam.

Year	Convergent Pedagogy school pupils' success rate	Classical French-based school pupils' success rate
1994	56.52	40.62
1995	37.64	42.34
1996	75.75	54.26
1997	50.00	36.89
1998	71.95	48.30
1999	78.75	49.13
2000	68.57	52.34

A 2004 statistical study conducted by the Division of Studies of Prediction and Evaluation, a sub-office of the National Centre of Exams and Competitions of the Ministry of Education, presents the statistics per Education Academy, the 7th grade entrance exam results of Medersas, Classical, and Convergent Pedagogy schools. The results show once more that Convergent Pedagogy schools perform higher (with a national rate of success of 70.36%) than Classical Schools (with a national rate of success of 56.52%), except for the Education Academy of Ségou where the classical ones perform better (53.18%) than the convergent pedagogy ones (52.58%). The table below gives deeper insight:

Table N°20:   Comparison of the 2004 results of Medersas, Classical and Convergent Pedagogy schools.

Education Academy	Convergent Pedagogy Schools' success rate in %	Classical Schools' success rate in %	Medersas' success rate in %
Bamako RD	81.14	66.33	63.52
Bamako RG	83.01	68.88	78.47
Kayes	81.62	52.70	74.96
Kita	//	51.22	51.22
Koulikoro	79.68	59.81	74.85
Kati	79.41	64.84	69.63
Sikasso	65.76	45.71	80.72
Koutiala	//	50.41	45.10
Ségou	52.58	53.18	48.23
San	73.60	54.09	75.54
Mopti	73.13	61.17	62.98
Douentza	//	50.22	
Timbuktu	//	69.24	
Gao	61.27	43.43	45.00
Kidal	//	65.55	
Total	70.36	56.52	58.99

The same division of the Ministry of Education conducted a similar statistical survey for 2005, and the results, though in progress for both school types, remain significantly high for bilingual schools. The results also indicate that even Medersas do slightly better than Classical schools.

Table N°21: Comparison of the 2005 results of Medersas, Classical and Convergent Pedagogy schools.

Education Academy	Convergent Pedagogy Schools' success rate in %	Classical Schools' success rate in %	Medersas' success rate in %
Bamako RD	84.06	63.77	66.69
Bamako RG	89.54	69.34	69.33
Kayes	80.10	62.88	68.15
Kita	84.28	59.07	86.77
Koulikoro	88.42	66.20	59.25
Kati	82.34	68.86	67.62
Sikasso	70.21	54.65	66.47
Koutiala	//	49.62	//
Ségou	76.11	52.85	47.15
San	73.97	56.71	57.45
Mopti	62.14	69.34	78.26
Douentza	//	67.01	//
Timbuktu	76.68	75.62	71.14
Gao	80.07	72.06	39.60
Kidal	//	76.92	//
Total	79.01	62.22	62.54

A deep analysis of the results shows a big difference in the rate of success between the two school types (classical and bilingual). And the table below presents the significance of that difference.

Table N°22: Illustration of the significance of the difference between the Convergent Pedagogy and the Classical systems.

Education Academy	Convergent Pedagogy Schools' success rate in %	Classical Schools' success rate in %	Difference
Bamako RD	84.06	63.77	20.29
Bamako RG	89.54	69.34	20.20
Kayes	80.10	62.88	17.22
Kita	84.28	59.07	25.21
Koulikoro	88.42	66.20	22.22
Kati	82.34	68.86	13.48
Sikasso	70.21	54.65	15.56
Koutiala	//	49.62	//
Ségou	76.11	52.85	23.26
San	73.97	56.71	17.26
Mopti	62.14	69.34	-7.20
Douentza	//	67.01	//
Timbuktu	76.68	75.62	01.06
Gao	80.07	72.06	08.01
Kidal	//	76.92	//
Total	79.01	62.22	16.79

The table above shows that Mopti is the only Academy in 2005 (with all the results taken into account) which has its classical schools performing higher than its Convergent Pedagogy ones. Again Mopti might be in the same situation as Timbuktu: Mopti is a crossroad between the north and the south, and has great tourist potentials. All the other academies present results significantly higher for Convergent Pedagogy schools.

In spite of all these happy conclusions in favour of Convergent Pedagogy, difficulties remain. Y. Haidara (2003, p.10) underlines the following problems:

the choice of the language of education in a multilingual area, the lack of teachers in general and for some national languages (Tamasheq, Soninké, Fulfuldé), the management of the teachers trained in convergent pedagogy, their pedagogical follow-up, and mainly the lack of didactic material, especially in the national languages.

These problems and several others have been (or are being) tackled by the government and its educational agencies (CNR-ENF, AMALAN, DNEB, etc.) through seminars and workshops. For instance, a dialect has been selected to serve as the standard form for each of the thirteen national languages; Teachers' training Institutes (IFM[36]) have been created to train more teachers for the schools; every year, national language specialists, bilingual teachers, academy advisors meet in Niono to develop didactic materials in the different languages. Bilingual teachers also receive training in reading, writing and teaching (in) the national languages.

This chapter has presented the steps in introducing the national languages in the Malian educational system and the legal framework which has allowed all that work to take place. It has specifically examined the results of the different phases of the experimentation of the national languages in formal education and the positive results achieved, which demonstrate the superiority of the bilingual schools over the classical ones. It has equally examined the Constitution in its articles which allow the use of mother tongue-based education and all the decrees, laws and ordinances which have permitted the country to use its native languages as media of instruction at school. But as a number of weaknesses have been underlined in the implementation of Convergent Pedagogy, an alternative approach, the Curriculum (of Basic Education, or to put it simply, the Curriculum Approach) has been proposed. The next chapter is devoted to that new methodology, in terms of its approach, strategies and advantages over Convergent Pedagogy.

---

[36] Institut de Formation des Maîtres (Teacher Training Institute)

Chapter six: The curriculum approach

The quest for quality education for citizens has been the priority of the government of Mali from the 1962 Reform to the 1998 educational system re-foundation. That can be seen in the different steps the basic education system has taken, moving from content-based education (Classical French-based system) to objective-based education (Convergent Pedagogy) and finally to competence-based education[37] (the Curriculum by Competence)[38]. It can also be seen in the different meetings which have been held in education (Mali, Ministère de l'Education Nationale. Actes du Forum National sur la généralisation du curriculum de l'enseignement fondamental des 9 et 10 septembre 2004, CNE, Division Nationale de l'Education de Base, p.17):

-*1962*: the Education Reform.

-*1964*: First National Seminar on Education.

-*1978*: Second National Seminar on Education.

-*1989*: General States of Education.

-*1991*: National Debate on Education.

-*1998*: The Education System Re-foundation.

It is in this framework that after years of practice and gradual expansion of Convergent Pedagogy, and after analysis of the weaknesses impeding its correct implementation and success, the Curriculum Approach has been proposed. One major feature of that Curriculum is that it is competence-based (i.e., integrated teaching). In the words of Y. Haidara (2006), the *Curriculum* is not an innovation as a number of people think it is: the Curriculum in its proper sense, has always characterised education; and that is why it is referred to as the Curriculum of Fundamental Education, which is nothing more than a new curriculum designed by the Ministry of National Education in order to gear education toward new demands and needs. What is new is the emphasis on the development of the learners' competences which are integrated. That is all the more sound that PRODEC has put among its priority areas the development of a new competence-based curriculum for basic education.

6.1. The Curriculum principles

As a pedagogical innovation, the Curriculum relies on a number of principles:

-Every child can and should succeed;

-There is interdisciplinarity;

-There is a need to foster autonomy in the child;

---

[37] Disciplinary, transversal, and life competences.
[38] Y. Haidara, Personal interview, 13/04/2006.

-The curriculum must be adapted to the learner's development and the evolution of the milieu; -It should guarantee the use of the mother tongue in formal education concomitantly with French (Mali, Ministèrede l'Education Nationale, Actes du Forum National sur la généralisation du curriculum de l'enseignement fondamental des 9 et 10 septembre 2004, CNE, Division Nationale de l'Education de Base, p.17).

6.2. Why the Curriculum?

The major reason for the Curriculum is that, there has been a need to gear education to the realities of the country and the current moment. There are three other reasons which are political, social and pedagogical.

-Political reasons: The advent of democracy necessitated a new type of citizen, patriot, and builder of his country, who perfectly knows his or her culture and who is open to the universal culture as well.

-Social reasons: The rise of new social demands with respect to education and practical training, useful to both the learners and their community.

-Pedagogical reasons: The de-compartmentalization of disciplines, training centred on the learner, and his real-life experiences and environment, the application of differentiated pedagogy at the level of the learners' achievements and rhythms of learning, and the link between theory and practice.

6.3. Advantages of the Curriculum Approach over Convergent Pedagogy

Advocates for the Curriculum approach maintain that it has the advantage of *"globalising learning activities in such a way as to ease the development of the skills necessary for the resolution of daily life problems"* (Mali, Ministère de l'Education Nationale, 2005, p.8). That was not the case in Convergent Pedagogy classes where there were no structured timetables. The table below shows the major differences between the two approaches:

Table N°23: Difference between Convergent Pedagogy and the Curriculum (adapted from Mali, Ministère de l'Education Nationale, 2005, p.8)

	Convergent Pedagogy	Curriculum
Aim		Identical
Programmes	Yearly objectives and pedagogical units	-Structured Programme -Presence of New Disciplines such as dancing, HS, Science in the 1st Year
Timetables	-Left to the teacher's initiative -Indication of the total class hours for each language	-The timetable: -Proposals of timetable scenarios -Indication of the total hours for each domain -Weekly planning
Educational Resources		Identical
Pedagogical Methods		Identical
Evaluation	-Formative Evaluation -Summative Evaluation	-Formative Evaluation -Summative Evaluation -Competence Evaluation

Basically, the unstructured Convergent Pedagogy pedagogical units have been replaced by the highly structured Curriculum learning units. A learning unit is a block which identifies the three competences, the objectives, the contents, and the learning and evaluation activities for each domain. It covers four weeks, three for acquisition and one for evaluation.

One principal difference between the two approaches observable from the table is the more structured timetable for the Curriculum. The Curriculum approach puts two timetable scenarios at the disposal of the classroom teacher (see the tables below). But whatever the timetable scenario the teacher selects, there should be no day without activities in language and communication (LC), science, mathematics and technology (SMT) and personal development (DP), and the time allocated to each subject should be respected.

Table N°24: First timetable scenario

Monday	Tuesday	Wednesday	Thursday	Friday
PD PSE	PD PSE	PD PSE	PD PSE	PD PSE
LC	LC	LC	LC	LC
PD CME	PD CME	PD CME	PD CME	PD CME
LC	LC	LC	LC	LC
SMT Math	SMT Math	SMT Math	SMT Math	SMT Math
LC	SMT MT	LC	LC	HS
Break	Break	Break	Break	Break
HS	HS			SMT ST
SMT ST	LC			LC
LC	Art			Art
Art	Support			Support

Table N°25: Second timetable scenario

Monday	Tuesday	Wednesday	Thursday	Friday
PD CME	PD PSE	PD CME	PD PSE	PD CME
LC		LC		
	LC		LC	LC
SMT Math	SMT Math	SMT Math	SMT Math	SMT Math
SMT ST		HS		PD PSE
	LC		LC	LC
SMT Math	Art	SMT Math	Art	SMT Math
LC	LC	LC	LC	LC
Break	Break	Break	Break	Break
LC	LC			
Art	HS			SMT ST
	LC			Art
LC	Support			Support

(Tables adapted from Mali, Ministère de l'Education Nationale, 2004, p.27).

In short, the Curriculum proposes to restore the learners to their central place in learning activities, and to provide teachers with approaches, methods, and adequate tools to inflect their practice, taking into account the needs of the pupils.

6.4. Competences in the Curriculum

The Curriculum is based on three central competences. In broader terms, a competence is defined as *"the sum of knowledge, good manners and know-how noticed and measured, enabling a person to accomplish in an adapted way, a task or a number of tasks"* (Ibid, p.12). In other words, it is a skill learned or acquired in a given field of knowledge.

i) Discipline-based competences: They are 24 and relate to the fields of training. Examples are:

-To express one's thought in a coherent and structured way in everyday life situations in writing;

-To manage one's environment;

-To express oneself with the body.

ii) Interdisciplinary competences: They are 6 and cover several training areas and are deployed in problem-solving activities. They can be intellectual, communicational, methodological, personal and social. Examples are:

-To react to communication;

-To co-operate;

-To adopt effective working methods.

iii) Life competences: They are 9 and express attitudes and behaviours essential for adaptation to life and serve to gear school to life. To put it plainly, they pertain to life experience and include health, social and economic activities, gender, child protection, leadership, etc. Examples include:

-To initiate and promote actions;

-To develop options to succeed in life;

-To participate in the up-keep and management of collective infrastructures.

What end profile is the new learner expected to develop?

The curriculum is organised around five principal domains which correspond to a series of five competences as displayed in the table below:

Table N°26: Domains and competences to develop in the learner.

Domains	Competences
L C (Languages and Communication)	To communicate orally and in writing, taking into account the communicative situation
S M T (Science, Mathematics and Technology)	To solve daily life problems
HS (Human Sciences)	To understand the world and fully take part in the development of one's country
Art	
PD (Personal Development)	To harmoniously integrate his milieu

Proponents of this pedagogical innovation perceive it as a *"strategy which considers each child in his cognitive, socio-affective and psycho-motor dimensions"* (ibid, p.4). But what basic advantages does the Curriculum have over Convergent Pedagogy?

6.5. Curriculum expansion steps: (from 2004-2005 to 2013-2014).

The generalisation of the Curriculum was decided by the Forum of Bamako held on the 9th and 10th of September 2004. The option chosen was a year to year expansion making use of a progressive and systemic strategy coupled with realism and caution.

Step I: Extension to convergent pedagogy schools

Given that the Curriculum departs from Convergent Pedagogy, the teaching of which a number of teachers have already acquired experience in (the use of active methods and national languages as both objects and medium of instruction), it appears in the eyes of the advocates for the innovation that Convergent Pedagogy schools should be the first to target. It was also meant to be implemented in all national languages and, in so doing, to uncover the possible constraints to its implementation.

Step II: Curriculum expansion

The second step involves the generalisation to all the first year classes of Level I in October 2005. The rest would be gradual.

Table N°27: Expansion of the new Curriculum of basic education (table adapted from Mali, Ministère de l'Education Nationale, 2004, p.12)

Level	Year	2004-05	2005-06	2006-07	2007-08	2008-09	2009-10	2010-11	2011-12	2012-13	2013-14	2014-15	2015-16
1	1												
	2												
2	3												
	4												
3	5												
	6												
4	7												
	8												
	9												

Curriculum expansion to Convergent Pedagogy schools.

Curriculum expansion to all schools.

The table above also shows that the Curriculum has four levels that correspond to nine classes. The first three levels correspond to the first six years of elementary school. The fourth level stands alone and corresponds to the three years of middle school.

Level I: 1st and 2nd grades.

Level II: 3rd and 4th grades.

Level III: 5th and 6th grades.

Level IV: 7th, 8th and 9th grades (middle school).

In fact, the (new) grade Curriculum organises education in Fundamental Education in a *block of nine years* corresponding respectively to *Initiation, Aptitude, Consolidation and Orientation*, and the five Training Domains (LC, SMT, PD, Art, and HS).

This chapter has presented the Curriculum as a competence-based approach. It has underlined the three basic competences underlying the methodology, namely, life, interdisciplinary and disciplined-based competences. It has also discussed the principles, the social, political and pedagogical reasons behind it and its advantages over Convergent Pedagogy. The chapter has equally examined the Curriculum expansion phases from 2004-2005 to 2015-2016, first to Convergent Pedagogy schools, then to the rest of the schools. It has finally discussed the two timetable scenarios put at the disposal of the teacher. The next chapter describes the attitudes of people in the commune of Gao towards the use of Songhay (their own mother tongue) as a medium of formal education for their children at school.

Chapter seven: Attitudes towards Songhay as a language of education in Gao

This chapter is the core of the research; it analyses the collected data and presents the findings per category of respondents, focusing on the the informants' attitudes expressed in terms of feelings, views, opinions, and perceptions about the use of their own language (Songhay) as a medium of instruction for their children at school. It further examines what the informants actually do, instead of what they just report vis-à vis the bilingual school system.

7.1. Headmasters' attitudes

Headmasters are the people in charge of the administration of education at the grassroot level in the sense that they are the ones who implement the government educational policies at the classroom level. Consequently, the determination of their feelings about such policies becomes highly significant.

As pointed out earlier, two headmasters from the two target schools constitute the sample at this level. Therefore, the determination of their feelings towards bilingual education becomes crucial in that they can foster or hamper the implementation of the system.

First, both headmasters have worked with both bilingual and classical teachers. That implies that the subjects are experienced and know much about mother tongue-based education, its advantages and drawbacks (if any) and teachers and parents' feelings about it. Secondly, they all feel satisfied with the results produced by both school systems. These answers are somewhat strange if we think about the seventh grade entrance exam results which always show that bilingual pupils outperform the classical ones. The responses could however be understood in the sense that while bilingual pupils perform better in the entrance exam, the classical ones do better starting from the seventh grade onward, a view commonplace among headmasters and teachers in the two schools[39]. That high performance of the classical products is possibly due to the total absence of the mother tongue and the teaching of all the subjects in the second language (French). Thirdly, the subjects would like to carry on working with teachers from both systems. As school admisistrators, they might not see any difference between the two teacher types as they should always put them on equal footing. That attitude could be explained by the fact that headmasters represent the government and implement the policy at the local level; they are subsequently expected to support everything the government back up. Fourth, while one informant indicated that he would accept to send his children to a bilingual school, the other would prefer a classical Frenchbased one for his children. The reason for such preferences may come from the fact that most people consider that bilingual

---

[39] Informal talks with the personnel of the two schools.

education is, in essence, good, but is being carried out under inadequate and inappropriate teaching and learning conditions, mainly teachers' lack of materials and training in teaching (in) the mother tongue. That was revealed during informal discussions with the teachers and headmasters after they filled out the questionnaire.

The headmasters' responses show that while they consider that they put both teacher types on equal footing, the bilingual teachers do not feel proud of the system they are working in, while the classical French-based ones do. In other words, bilingual teachers work in a system they do not like; that indicates that the system has been imposed upon them because all the schools of the commune have turned bilingual. It might also be that they were not initially trained as teachers, but have become so because of the shortage of teachers. Another reason for this sentiment on the part of bilingual teachers, as contended by headmasters, might come from the fact that they complain more than their classical counterparts about their difficult working conditions and their lack of adequate teaching materials. But, is the lack of didactic materials not a general problem facing all teachers?

The headmasters equally postulate that both wealthy people and educated ones send their children, not to bilingual, but to classical French-based schools. One can easily understand that wealthy people send their children to classical private schools (there are no more classical public schools in the commun) because on the one hand, they have the financial resources to do so, but on the other hand, they often lack the kind of knowledge required to understand the relationships between language and education. But educated people should be the first to embrace bilingual education.

In fact, it looks as if people in the commune of Gao, both un-/educated people, perceive education as the acquisition of elitist knowledge in an elitist language (French). Such a feeling appears all the more true that both wealthy people and educated ones send or would like to send their children to French-based schools. In the eyes of such people, to go to school means to go to learn French and to study science in French. That implies that Songhay is not an elitist language they like their children to learn and to study in. Songhay is the language of the layman, a language which lacks all the advantages that French has. But have people been informed and convinced about the issue of bilingual education?

The answer is rather negative. In the view of one subject, people adhere to bilingual education and thinks that the system will have a bright future but with the condition *"if it continues up to junior high school,"*; the other subject contends just the reverse, i. e., people do not adhere to the system, and the system will not have a bright future because of lack of information and consciousness-raising. It is worth noting here that the proponents of the bilingual approach propose that it continues through high school. But for the time being, that has not been the case. In short, the respondents agree that for the time being, the bilingual system in Mali does not or will not have a bright future as it does not go beyond elementary school.

The two respondents have divergent views about the benefits of bilingual education: while one believes that it is beneficial for a pupil to be the product of bilingual education, the other supports just the opposite view, but both recognise that decentralisation opens up job opportunities for the bilingual products.

In sum, the subjects agree on the following points: bilingual teachers have developed a low image of themselves and their education system; they do not have enough didactic materials, and complain more than their classical counterparts. Both wealthy people and educated ones send their children only to classical private schools. And decentralisation opens up job opportunities for the bilingual products. The rest of the responses are rather balanced: positive for one informant and negative for the other. It is true that the subjects do not show that they have negative attitudes toward the bilingual system, but they note that their pupils' parents and teachers do.

7.1.1. Headmasters' behaviours

Earlier, in this analysis of the headmasters' attitudes, one informant indicated that if he had children to send to school, he would send them to a classical school rather than a bilingual one. The same subject is stating now that he has children who all attend the classical school system. So, he does not make an exception to all those educated people who, in his view, send their children to the classical French-based system. At this level, there is a correlation between what the informant says and what he does. Unfortunately, the other respondent, who indicated that he would send his children to either school if he had children to send, does not have any. Consequently, he did not answer the other basic questions on the school type the children go to. But the responses show that negative behaviour is likely to prevail among the subjects, a behaviour which looks all the more surprising that headmasters are usually considered as the engine driving bilingual education.

The headmasters have reported the attitudes of classroom practioners (the teachers) about the bilingual system. It will be insightful to ask the teachers to report their own feelings about the use of Songhay as a medium of instruction. The next section is devoted to this task.

7.2. Teachers' attitudes

This section analyses teachers' attitudes at Gaday A and Faranjiray B on the use of Songhay in their schools. Eighteen (18) teachers were administered the questionnaire. The teacher group was divided into two sub-groups: classical and bilingual. Recognising their differences in terms of (re-)training, curriculum type, and timetables, the researcher has designed separate questionnaires for the two groups. Four (4) subjects in the group are classical French-based teachers from Gaday A. That school introduced bilingual education in its system in 2003. The other fourteen subjects (14) are bilingual teachers from both Gaday A and Faranjiray B.

7.2.1. Classical French-based teachers' attitudes

The four (4) respondents of this category have already used the classical teaching method; three among them would like to carry on using this method which they find superior to the bilingual one because, in their eyes, the pupils perform better starting from the seventh grade. The other informant did not answer the question though he looks experienced enough in teaching (10 years) to make a decision. He assumes that the pupils do not learn better when the teaching medium is French only, and sustains that they learn better under the bilingual system.

It is noteworthy that none of the four informants were initially trained as a teacher; in fact, an analysis of their background shows that three of them were holders of a CAP[40] diploma in agriculture. One of them did not want to tell the researcher his diploma (if any): the informant belongs to that group of 'teachers' who do not hold any diploma. The subjects' preference for classical teaching comes from their lack of competence in terms of diploma and/or required training, especially in national language teaching. Had they graduated from teachers' training colleges or institutes, they would have opted differently.

Proceeding further, all the respondents agree that language is a factor in the development of a country; but three (75%) sustain that French can play that role. The perception behind that answer might also be that in their eyes, French is an elitist language giving people access to elitist knowledge. Consequently, these three teachers are also proud to be elitist teachers sharing elitist knowledge in an elitist language.

Table N°28: Classical French based teachers' pride towards the classical teaching method.

Are you proud to know and teach in French only?			
Yes		No	
n°	%	n°	%
3	75	1	25

---

[40] Certificat d'Aptitude Professionnelle (Certificate of Professional Aptitude).

The other informant (the same as in the above analysis) posits that only Songhay can play that role and that he would be proud to know and teach in Songhay, rather than in French.

The same three respondents indicate that the French medium opens up equal opportunities to all Malian children while the other posits the reverse. Two informants add that it fosters elitism (it favors an educated minority). The answers of these two subjects look contradictory: on the one hand, they maintain that the French medium gives equal opportunities to all Malian children; on the other hand, they maintain that it favors a minority group.

The classical teachers in their majority find that they are on an equal footing with the bilingual ones. One of them supports the opposite view. Nevertheless, all of them think that they are equal to their bilingual counterparts who, in their turn, express the same feeling.

Lastly, the same majority (75%) believe that the products of the classical school system have advantages over their bilingual counterparts, and defend that the classical system has a bright future in Mali. Unfortunately, these teachers are on the verge of disappearing with the system they are defending. The converse view is held by one teacher. The table below sums-up their teachers' responses.

Table N°29: Classical teachers' feelings towards the bilingual ones.

Do you feel ……………..to your bilingual fellows?						Do your bilingual fellows show that they're………………….to you?					
Inferior to		Equal to		Superior to		Inferior to		Equal to		Superior to	
n°	%	n°	%	n°	%	n°	%	n°	%	n°	%
0	0	4	100	0	0	0	0	4	100	0	0

7.2.1.1. Classical French-based teachers' behaviours

The subjects making up the group all have children who go to school. Three of them (75%) (the same who stated earlier that they preferred classical to bilingual education) have their children in private schools where the classical French-based system is used, and where they have to pay tuition fees; distance, wind, heat, money and other negative factors do not prevent them from sending their children to classical schools. One informant indicates that his children go to bilingual schools because he likes such schools. Shortly put, negative behaviour towards the use of Songhay appears dominant among classical teachers.

On the whole, the data analysis in this section displays that the majority of the classical teachers have positive images of themselves and of their French based-system; such attitudes may stem from their perception of what 'education'is: the acquisition of elitist knowledge in an elitist language.

7.2.2. Bilingual teachers' attitudes

This teacher subgroup includes fourteen (14) subjects eleven (11) of whom (78.57%) have already taught in the bilingual system, while three others (21.43%) have not. But they all teach in the same bilingual schools. The three teachers follow the classical French based-system in the bilingual school as they have not yet received training in teaching in the mother tongue (as the others have). They have come to teach because of the teacher shortage, so have been hired under very particular circumstances: they are agriculture CAP diploma holders. That is not the case of the seven other subjects (50%) who received initial teacher training and who are IPEG[41] diploma holders. In plain words, only half of the bilingual teachers were initially trained as teachers. The other half comes from various sectors with various qualifications (for instance, mechanics, agriculture, etc.).

When pupils' parents become aware of this state of affairs prevailing in schools, they just go and withdraw their children from bilingual schools and send them to the private classical ones which are thought to be 'better'. In fact, people do not complain very much about bilingual education itself, but rather the conditions under which it is implemented: if only half of the teachers had received initial teacher training, the pupils who are taught by the other half would certainly be less lucky in terms of the quality of the education they receive.

It is important to note that two out of those three teachers, plus four others (42.85%) coming from those who used to teach in Songhay, do not want to continue teaching in the bilingual system. One subject did not answer the question. The other seven subjects (50%) would like to keep on teaching in Songhay. That implies that the majority of the bilingual teachers appreciate the methodology.

Table N°30: Bilingual teachers' perceptions of bilingual education.

Would you like to keep on teaching in the bilingual system?					
Yes		No		No answer	
n°	%	n°	%	n°	%
7	50	6	42.85	1	7.14

---

[41] Institut Pedagogique d'Enseignement Général (Teacher Training School)

The issue of teaching conditions has been stressed by most bilingual teachers (64.28%) who consider that they do not have adequate didactic materials for their classes. The rest of the subjects (35.71%) think that they do.

The importance of using Songhay as a medium of instruction has been emphasised by the majority of bilingual teachers (64.28%) who believe that pupils learn better under the bilingual approach, a feeling which is in line with the results of the studies carried out to compare the two systems. At this level, it clearly appears that the majority of bilingual teachers defend the superiority of bilingual education over the classical one; but it is useful to signal that the same majority asserted earlier that there were no adequate teaching materials. So the point to make is that bilingual education is good in theory, but is poorly implemented: the current teaching conditions are inadequate. That perception goes hand in hand with one headmaster's statement which asserts that bilingual education is superior to the classical French based one provided that the teaching conditions are improved; and he sadly recognises that that has not been the case. In plain words, for the time being, it remains ineffective as a teaching/learning methodology. Five respondents (35.71%) only recogninse the superiority of the classical system when they ascertain that pupils learn better under that system. That attitude is supported by eight respondents (57.14%) who maintain that bilingual education does not reduce the rate of school failure (at least not in its current form); but, six others (42.85%) think that it does. Nevertheless, there seems to be a contradiction in these last responses in the sense that the majority of the teachers cannot at the same time support a viewpoint and its opposite: in fact, nine bilingual subjects (64.28%) have stated that learners perform better in bilingual education and the converse view is supported by nearly the same majority (57.14%). Such a contradiction might stem from the misunderstanding of the questions put. But their background of the information uncovers that the subjects are experienced and are susceptible of comprehending average language. But, as one headmaster highlighted, the advantage for bilingual pupils is, without question, the use of the mother tongue. In fact, starting from the seventh grade, the classical pupils appear to outperform the bilingual ones because they have been in the second language right from the beginning and because of the wider availability of teaching materials in that language.

Table N°31: The effectiveness of bilingual education.

Pupils perform better in the bilingual system				Bilingual education reduces the rate of school drop-out			
yes		No		Yes		no	
n°	%	n°	%	n°	%	n°	%
9	64.28	5	35.71	6	42.85	8	57.14

Moving further with the importance of using Songhay in science, nine respondents (64.28%) think that this language cannot express most scientific concepts; Three other respondents (21.42%) sustain that it can and even contend that it allows true mastery of science subjects such as mathematics and biology. Two people (14.28%) did not answer. The responses provided suggest that Songhay needs further research for standardisation, dictionary-making, borrowing, etc. (status and corpus planning); and the work is being conducted by AMALAN.[42]

It was noted earlier that eight bilingual teachers (57.14%) defended that their system does not reduce the rate of school failure. It follows that ten subjects (71.42%) are asserting now that the bilingual system is not meant for poor families (as well to do families are said to send their children to classical French-based private schools); and eight others (57.14%) argue that it does not weaken the learners' level of education. Their attitudes are contradicted by those of four other teachers (28.57%) who think that the bilingual system is meant for poor families, and also by another group of six respondents (42.85%) who defend that it weakens the learners' level of education. So, the subjects' responses at this level rather show balanced attitudes.

Most bilingual teachers (78.57%) also believe that language can be a factor for the development of a country, while only a handful (35.71%) considers that Songhay can play that role. Three teachers (21.42%) refute the view that language can be a development factor and six other informants (42.85%) support that Songhay cannot play that role, but French can.

---

[42] Interview with P. Guindo on:

96

Table N°32: Negative attitudes towards the use of Songhay as a factor of development in Mali.

Can language be a factor for the development a country?				Can Songhay play that role?			
yes		*No*		*yes*		*no*	
n°	%	n°	%	n°	%	n°	%
11	78.57	3	21.42	5	35.71	6	42.85

In fact, though bilingual teachers seem to like and defend the Songhay language, and would like to see it preserved as a medium of instruction, most of them do not think that that language can ensure the development of the country. That attitude is in line with the perception displayed earlier by the nine bilingual informants (64.28%) who asserted that Songhay is not a language of science.

A significant element brought about in this analysis is that most pupils' parents have not been informed about the methodology. It looks as if there is a lack of awareness-raising on the part of the educational authorities. That view is held by ten respondents (71.42%) who also posit that parents do not adhere to the approach, and eight other teachers (57.14%) who assert that they have not been informed and convinced. The point is that most parents who have heard about bilingual education think that children go to school to study and learn Songhay over which (in their eyes) they already have full command. Most other people have not even heard about it yet, though they have their children in those bilingual schools.

A few teachers (28.57%) maintain that parents are informed about the issue; a handful (14.28%) ascertains that parents adhere to the system; two subjects (14.28%) did not answer. The table below illustrates.

Table N°33: People's level of awareness-raising and information about bilingual education.

Are parents informed about bilingual educatio				Do they adhere to the approach ?						If they do not, is it because of lack of:			
yes		no		yes		No		No answer		Information		Awareness-raising	
n°	%	n°	%	n°	%	n°	%	n°	%	n°	%	n°	%
4	28.57	10	71.42	2	14.28	10	71.42	2	14.28	8	57.14	8	57.14

A look at how French is perceived by bilingual teachers reveals that most informants (57.14%) believe that language can be a factor in the development of a country and that French (rather than Songhay) can play that role. Those respondents seem to ignore or disagree with the commonly held view that *no country can develop on the sole basis of a foreign language.* Another group (64.28%) defends that French used as a medium of education helps guarantee equal opportunities to all Malian children. Three (21.42%) among them consider that French cannot develop Mali, but at the same time maintain that it offers equal opportunities to all the children of the country. That is not the perception held by another group of subjects (57.14%) who believe that knowledge of French ensures elitism, i.e., the mastery of that language offers a minority group advantages over the majority group.

The overwhelming majority (78.57%) of bilingual teachers supports that classical French based teaching has a bright future in Mali. That assumption might stem from their disapproval for bilingual education or from the fact that there are a growing number of parents who withdraw their children from public bilingual schools and send them to the classical French-based private ones. They might also have the feeling that the local school authorities who defend the methodology send their children, not to bilingual schools, but to the private ones. The consequence of such feelings might be that, sooner or later, the methodology will be abandoned, and there will be a comeback to the classical system.

On the other hand, six respondents (42.85%) consider that French alone cannot be a factor which helps develop a country. That attitude is supported by five subjects (35.71%) who equally point out that French as the sole education medium does not offer the same opportunities to all Malian children. Few subjects (28.57%) maintain that that language ensures elitism to a minority. Two informants (14.28%) did not answer; but three (21.42%) assume that the classical French based teaching system does not have any (good) future.

Proceeding further in the analysis, the findings uncover that half of the bilingual informants (50%) equally believe that the products of the classical French-based system have advantages over their bilingual counterparts; that appears all the more sound that the pupils who benefit from the classical system receive education in an elitist language. Only three among them (21.42%) support that bilingual products have advantages over the classical ones. But, four (28.57%) did not answer, possibly because they do not have a clear idea about the issue. Only a survey on the future occupation of both kinds of pupils could truly inform about the advantages of either group.

However, eleven informants (78.57%) argue that teachers who have been trained in Songhay are operational in decentralisation, while two others (14.28%) think that they are not; one did not answer. In plain words, most subjects consider that their category is ready for use in decentralisation. But, on the whole, the majority of bilingual teachers have expressed negative attitudes towards the bilingual system they use.

7.2.2.1. Bilingual teachers' lack of pride

Most bilingual teachers (57.14%) do not feel proud of their Songhay-based medium of instruction, and would rather be proud of the French one. In addition, they would not choose to teach in Songhay had they to do it all over again, i.e., they prefer the classical French-based system. Six teachers (42.85%) feel proud of the Songhay medium of instruction and would choose it had they to do it all over again. It is worthy to note that twelve subjects (85.71%) out of fourteen have received training in bilingual education.

Table N°34: The bilingual teachers' lack of pride towards the Songhay-based medium of instruction.

Are you proud to teach in Songhay?				Would you choose to teach in Songhay, had you to do it all over again?			
Yes		no		yes		No	
n°	%	n°	%	n°	%	n°	%
6	42.85	8	57.14	6	42.85	8	57.14

One significant element that the analysis of these responses has revealed is that the school administration does not seem to create any discrimination among the teachers. The view is supported by twelve teachers (85.71%) who ascertain that they are put on equal footing with their classical counterparts. That is backed up by ten informants (71.42%) who argue that they feel equal to their classical counterparts whom they believe share the same feeling towards them.

A few teachers (14.28%) do not feel equal to their French-based felows. In support, two informants (14.28%) feel superior to their classical counterparts and two others (14.28%) feel inferior to their classical fellows. Only three subjects (21.42%) argue that classical teachers think that they are superior to them (bilinguals).

7.2.2.2. Bilingual teachers' bahaviours

The analysis of the findings displays that twelve informants (85.71%) have children who go to school. Seven of them (58.33%) have their children in the classical schools only. And three subjects from the same group (25%) have children in both systems. Two respondents (14.21%) have children in the bilingual schools only. Two other bilingual subjects (14.21%), who do not have children at school, did not answer.

It clearly appears from the above figures that the majority of bilingual teachers whatever their underlying reasons, prefer the classical schools for their children, even if they have to send them to private French-based classical schools where there are school fees to pay. Few among them prefer to adopt a clever attitude, i.e., sharing the children between the two systems.

As for the true reasons behind those choices, five subjects (41.66%) whose children go to school (58.33%) have a preference for the classical system, while two informants from the same group (6.66%) have their choice guided by the distance factor. As to the three respondents who have children in either school system, they have expressed different reasons: one informant prefers the bilingual system, a second one prefers the classical one, and a third one likes both systems with distance as the major factor. Lastly, the two teachers who have children in the bilingual system sustain that their children attend that system just because they (the teachers) prefer it. In short, bilingual teachers, just like the classical ones, have a negative behaviour toward the use of Songhay as a medium of instruction.

In sum, this analysis has shown that the majority of bilingual teachers do not like the approach, but they do not suffer any discrimination neither from the school administration, nor from their classical fellows. The informants have expressed the superiority of bilingual education, but at the same time, have stressed the inadequate and inappropriate implementation conditions.

One further aspect which this research needs to disclose is how the pupils who undergo the innovation feel about it. That is the subject of the next section.

7.3. Pupils' attitudes

This section analyses the pupils' attitudes towards bilingual education. Like the group of teachers, the group of pupils is made up of two sub-groups: the classical and the bilingual.

7.3.1. Classical French-based pupils' attitudes

The significance of the determination of the pupils' feelings towards educational systems is crucial since the pupils are the subjects who undergo experimentation and who will be the products of the innovation.

An examination of the findings discloses that all the eight informants like to study (or continue to study) in French only, not in Songhay. However, six pupils (75%) understand just a little bit (not much) what their teacher says in French, while two others (25%) understand everything s/he says.

The informants' responses with regard to arithmetic are rather balanced. In fact, four subjects (50%) understand everything the teacher gives them in arithmetic and four others (50%) understand just a little bit. These answers evidently demonstrate that the pupils feel more at ease in arithmetic than in general French.

The subjects are all proud of themselves and the type of school they attend. In other words, the pupils would not be proud of bilingual schools and therefore would not like to go to such a type of school. That attitude is supported by five respondents (62.5%) who believe that they are superior to their bilingual fellows, while three others (38.5%) think that they are equal to them. Besides, seven informants (87.5%) also consider that their bilingual friends think that they (the classical pupils) are superior to them because of the French language in which they study. One informant only (12.5%) thinks that they are all equal.

Table N°35: The classical French-based pupils' negative attitudes towards bilingual education.

Do you think that you are----to your bilingual counterparts?					
Superior to?		Equal to?		Inferior to?	
5	62.5%	3	38.5%	0	0%

Following the same general trend, five respondents (62.5%) freely chose to go to the classical French-based school system, while three others (38.5%) were sent there by their families. No pupils were forced to attend the classical system. Finally, all the subjects would like to continue in the classical school system; and more significantly, they would all choose to go to a classical school, had they to do it all over again. Shortly put, the overwhelming majority of the classical pupils like their school type, have a particular preference for it, feel definitely proud of it and would all like to continue in it.

7.3.2. Bilingual pupils' attitudes

The previous section has uncovered that nearly all the informants in the classical system have expressed their pride and preference for this system. This section analyses the bilingual pupils' feelings towards the use of Songhay as a medium of instruction.

There are twenty-one bilingual subjects interviewed. Fifteen (71.42%) do not like the bilingual programme they have followed so far and consequently prefer the classical one. The remaining six other pupils (28.57%) prefer their bilingual programme and by the same token reject the classical system. Additionally, seventeen pupils (80.95%) understand everything the teacher says in Songhay, while six others (28.57%) understand everything s/he says in French (both languages are used at this level). That is all the more sound that the teacher lectures in the pupils' mother tongue. A smaller group of five subjects (23.80%) understand a little bit what the teacher says in Songhay, ten others (47.61%) understand just a little bit what the teacher says in French. Three first year pupils (14.28%) did not answer, possibly because of their younger age. Another first year respondent just does not understand anything the teacher says in French.

Proceeding further in the analysis, the researcher discovers that fourteen informants (66.66%) understand everything when the teacher explains arithmetic in Songhay, while eleven pupils (52.38%) comprehend everything the teacher says in arithmetic in French. Six respondents (28.57%) however understand just a little bit what the teacher says in Songhay; five people (23.80%) understand a little bit arithmetic when the teacher explains in French. Four first year informants (19.04%) did not respond. These last figures obviate that the level of comprehension looks higher with bilingual subjects (80.95%) than with the classical ones (25%), at least in beginning classes.

Looking at the very feelings of the pupils towards bilingual education, the researcher notices that seventeen subjects (80.95%) definitely do not feel proud of the bilingual programme they have been following, and would be proud of a classical French-based one. Only four informants (19.04%) feel proud of themselves and the school type they go to. The plain truth is that most pupils and pupils' parents do not have the choice of school type as bilingual education has been extended to all the public schools of the Commune of Gao. And the very few *wealthy* people in the Commune prefer to send their children to private classical schools.

Table N°36: Bilingual pupils' lack of pride vis-à-vis bilingual education

Do you feel proud to be in a bilingual school?			
Yes		No	
4	19.04%	17	80.95%

Following the same trend, eleven pupils (52.38%) do not feel inferior or superior, but equal to the classical ones, but eight others (38.09%) feel inferior to them, and one feels (4.76%) superior. It however follows that the pupils themselves do not seem to discriminate very much or mock at each other because of a given school type that one attends. For sixteen subjects (76.19%) confess that their classical counterparts do not care about the school type they follow, while four others (19.04%) ascertain that the classical ones do. One first year subject did not answer the questions related to the feelings of inferiority, equality and superiority. But the same pupil also finds that the classical ones mock at them because of the Songhay language.

Table N°37: Bilingual pupils' perception by their classical fellows.

Do you think you are----your classical fellows?					
Superior to?		Equal to?		Inferior to?	
1	4.76%	11	52.38%	8	38.09%

Bilingual pupils were not, in general, forced to attend the school type they attend. That view is supported by nine respondents (42.85%) who freely chose to go to a bilingual school. In fact, there was no choice of school to make because when the pupils went to school for the first time, bilingual education was already extended to all the public schools of the commune. The subjects probably chose the closest school, but not a specific school type. Nevertheless, seven other pupils (33.33%) sustain that they were sent to school by their families. Again the reasons behind the parents' choice of a school type is not always easy to determine because of factors like distance, extension of the bilingual methodology, or the parents' lack of awareness about the existence of bilingual education in their schools. Thus, pupils were just sent to school. But, very explicitly pointed out, four respondents (19.04%) were forced by their parents to attend a bilingual school. A fourth year pupil even openly confesses *"I am ashamed of Songhay"*. One last pupil did not answer.

Bilingual pupils (80.95%) have indicated earlier that they do not feel proud of their school type and do not want to continue their studies in such a school type. They (80.95%) would also choose to go to a classical school, had they to do it all over again. More, fourteen respondents (66.66%) believe that they are not well perceived by people when they tell them that they study in bilingual schools. In converse, four subjects (19.04%) want to continue in their bilingual schools and therefore would choose to go to such a school, had they to di it all over again. Six others (28.57%) consider that they are well perceived by people when they tell them that they are in a bilingual school. There is still one student who did not answer the last question.

Table N°38: Bilingual pupils' preference to the classical French-based system.

Which school type would you choose to go to, had you to?			
Classical school?		Bilingual school?	
16	76.19%	4	19.04%

On the whole, this analysis has shown that while bilingual instruction tends to be more effective and superior to the classical one, possibly because of the use of the pupils' mother tongue and the training that the teachers receive (first in French, then in the mother tongue), the overwhelming majority of the bilingual subjects interviewed have expressed their dislike, disapproval, shame, and lack of pride vis-à-vis that pedagogical innovation, and by the same token, advocates the classical French-based system. The findings yielded by the two pupil groups have demonstrated that the majority of both classical and bilingual pupils advocate the classical French-based educational system, and thereby, reject the bilingual system. More, bilingual pupils seem to have developed a negative image of themselves because of that school bilingualism. Only lower class citizens continue to send their children to public bilingual schools. Middle and upper class people send their children to private classical schools. That is all the more understandable that it is a novelty and old habits die hard. An effective strategy to fight against such a situation is to continue to inform, raise awareness and create an enjoyable learning environment for both pupils and teachers.

Teachers, headmasters and pupils are all key school stakeholders whose views are crucial in the implemention of language policy and planning. Other important school partners include NGOs working in the sector of education. The next section is devoted to that question.

7.4. NGO representatives' attitudes

The selected Non-Governmental Organisations work in the education sector in partnership with primary schools and are aware of the schools' introduction of bilingual education. For instance, the activities of SEAD involve two components: a) teacher training and; b) support to the Curriculum. Like most NGOs in the commune, SEAD is represented at the CAP[43] of Gao. World Education in particular works in the field of community participation, empowerment, and capacity building. The NGO works in partnership with SMC, PTA, and CMA members. On the whole, the two NGO education representatives are well involved in education matters in the Commune of Gao.

The NGO representatives interviewed find that (the introduction of) bilingual education is a good thing, defend its superiority over the classical one and appear definitely favourable to it. They generally work as advisors to the school administration and take part in the implementation of the policy through teacher training. As active school partners, the

---

[43] Centre d'Animation Pedagogique (Pedagogical Animation Centre, the new terminology for the Inspectorate)

respondents know about the strengths and weaknesses of the approach. That justifies the perceptions they have expressed.

The subjects would all send their children to the classical school type, had they to do it all over again. But one of them would equally send them to the bilingual type, too. That implies that that subject does not make any distinction between the two types of school. The table below illustrates the feelings about bilingual education.

Table N°39: Attitudes of NGOs towards bilingual education.

Items	Yes		No	
	Number	%	Number	%
Is bilingual education a good thing?	2	100	0	0
Do pupils do better in bilingual education?	2	100	0	0
Are you in favour of bilingual education?	2	100	0	0
Would you advise the school administration to use bilingual education?	2	100	0	0

While NGO representatives advocate the bilingual education system, people in the commune are rather reluctant. Thus, the respondents agree that people do not adhere to the approach and that is because they have not been informed, nor made aware about the methodology. They equally admit that both wealthy people and educated ones definitely prefer to send their children, not to bilingual schools, but to the classical ones, as illustrated in the table below.

Table N°40: People's feelings towards bilingual education according to NGO representatives.

Items	Yes		No	
	Number	%	Number	%
People adhere to bilingual education	0	0	2	100
If no, because of lack of information and awareness-raising	2	100	0	0
Wealthy parents send children to classical schools	2	100	0	0
Educated people send children to classical schools	2	100	0	0

7.4.1. NGO representatives' behaviour

This section examines possible correlations between what NGO representatives report as attitudes and how they actually behave. All the informants have children who go to school, no matter the type of school (bilingual or classical). More, they all have children in the classical school type; but, one of them also has children in the bilingual one. That clearly indicates that one informant seems to have confidence (at least for the time being) in the classical type only, while the other tends to have confidence in either type. It is good to indicate that there are parents who are not very confident in the schooling system; therefore they prefer to try either system. During informal talks, the informants have disclosed that in fact, bilingual education is good in theory, but the conditions under which it is implemented turn it *bad*. They argue that it activates thinking and learning and uses resources from the learner's own social environment. But its implementation requires information, preparation, consciousness-raising, and home follow up. They also agree that it is a tool for local development. But, on the whole, negative behaviour definitely prevails among NGO representatives.

In sum, the findings in this section have displayed that NGOs have positive attitudes towards bilingual education. The informants have recognised the superiority of the approach, but have also admitted that its current implementation conditions cause it to fail. The analysis has also shown that people in general, particularly educated and the wealthy ones have an aversion to bilingual education.

Another significant category of informants among school partners to consider remains the PTA, SMC and CMA members. They form groups of school stakeholders whose involvement in school affairs can be seen in terms of their contributions in decision-making and the orientations they propose to school authorities. The next section is dedicated to the analysis of their feelings towards the use of Songhay as a medium of instruction.

7.5. School Management Committee, Parent Teachers Association and Child Mother Association members' attitudes

This section describes the perceptions, feelings, opinions and the points of views of some key school stakeholders. The group is made up of seventeen subjects. It is also worth noting that though the group is made up of three categories, the members have received the same questionnaire, and the data has been analysed as a whole.

The findings show that eleven informants (64.70%) would not send their children to a bilingual school, but to a classical one, had they to do it all over again. Five respondents (29.41%) would not make a difference between the two types of school and would therefore send their children to either type. One informant (5.88%) among those five does not have children in a bilingual school, but in the classical one. Thus, there seems to be a contradiction between what the informant states and what s/he does. Only one informant (5.88%) would send his children to a bilingual school.

As to the relationships between bilingual education and successful future career, nine respondents (52.94%) believe that the bilingual products will not easily get a job and that bilingual education will not lead to successful future life. In converse, six others (35.29%) support the opposite view. Eight subjects (47.05%) find that the bilingual products will not be jobless, but seven (41.17%) think that they will. There are two informants who did not answer.

Supporting this general trend, fourteen informants (82.35%) sustain that the classical school products will easily get a job and will have a successful life; but three others did not respond. Proceeding further, nine subjects (52.94%) hold that it is a good thing to study in the classical schools, while another group of eight informants (47.05%) consider that it is a good thing to study in either school system. In other words, in the eyes of that last group, both school types are equal or at least, are equally perceived by those respondents. The table below summarises the respondents' feelings.

Table N°41: Feelings about the impact of bilingual education on learners' careers.

			Yes	6	35.29%
If you send a child to a bilingual school	s/he will easily get a job		No	9	52.94%
			No answer	2	11.76%
	s/he will succeed in life		Yes	6	35.29%
			No	9	52.94%
			No answer	2	11.76%
	s/he will be jobless		Yes	7	41.17%
			No	8	47.05%
			No answer	2	11.76%
If you send a child to a classical school	s/he will easily get a job		Yes	14	82.35%
			No	0	0%
			No answer	3	17.64%
	s/he will succeed in life		Yes	14	82.35%
			No	0	0%
			No answer	3	17.64%
	s/he will be jobless		yes	0	0%
			No	14	82.35%
			No answer	3	17.64%

Nevertheless, fourteen informants (82.35%) recognise that it is advantageous to study in the Songhay-based bilingual system; seven subjects (41.17%) find the advantages to be cultural only, and seven others (41.17%) find them to be both cultural and financial. In other words, the prevailing feelings among the respondents are that the basic significance of studies in Songhay lies in the preservation of the cultural values underlying the language. That opinion is all the more true that the mastery of Songhay is not a requirement for working in the civil service. One subject did not answer.

On the other hand, sixteen informants (94.11%) find it advantageous to study in the classical French-based system. One subject only finds no advantage, while two others (11.76%) did not answer. The reasons expressed are diverse: fourteen people (82.35%) support that studying in French has both financial and cultural advantages. Two other informants (11.76%) emphasise the financial aspect as the only advantage as that language is the only medium in the public administration. One person did not answer. So the respondents at this level put more stress on the financial advantage that studying in French procures than on the one that Songhay can provide. Such an attitude can be explained by the fact that every civil servant must have a full command over French.

Table N°42: Informants' feelings vis-à-vis the classical school system.

Is it a good thing to study in :					
Classical schools?		Bilingual schools?		Both classical and bilingual schools?	
Number	%	Number	%	Number	%
9	52.94	0	0	8	47.05

A closer look at the subjects' responses suggests that the pedagogical assumption behind bilingual education is not very much the one perceived by the respondents. In fact, the majority of the informants find that the basic advantages behind the bilingual approach are the preservation of the Songhay cultural identity. But the advantages for studying in French are both financial and cultural with the former taking on the latter. Whatever the hidden or apparent reasons behind those feelings, the wider majority of the subjects (82.35%) do not regret the type of school in which they have sent their children; that is probably because those children have been able to learn how to read and write. Regarding unemployment, it can be seen as a general concern, regardless of the type of school attended and training received. Three informants (17.64%) did not answer.

A significant number of subjects, however (47.05%) are proud to have sent their children to a classical school; four others (23.52%) are proud to have sent their children to either school type; one (5.88%), a restaurant owner, is proud to have sent her child to a bilingual school; four (23.52%) did not answer.

7.5.1. School Management Committee, Parent Teachers Association and Child Mother Association members' behaviours

This section determines the school type the children of key school stakeholders that the PTA, SMC and CMA members constitute go to, and consequently, to set a relationship between what those subjects report and how they act. Thus, sixteen respondents (94.11%) out seventeen have children; twelve (70.58%) among them have children who go to school, and five (29.41%) have no children who go to school. Nine others (52.94%) have their children in the classical school system (possibly because they do not like the bilingual educational system). Four other subjects (23.52%) have children in either school type (adopting the pragmatic attitude that if one school type does not produce good results, the other will). Another group of four subjects (23.52%) have no children at school (at least, not in basic education as the respondents have all retired). A last informant, the pupils' representative at the School Management Committee (fourteen years old), did not answer. But the findings, wholly examined, demonstrate that negative behaviour towards bilingual education prevails among PTAs, SMCs and CMAs (52.94%) as illustrated in the table below.

Table N°43: SMC, PTA and CMA members' behaviour towards bilingual education

Items	Yes		No	
	Number	%	Number	%
Children attend bilingual school only	0	0	9	52.94
Children attend classical school only	9	52.94	0	0
Children are shared between the two school types	4	23.52	0	0

In short, the findings of this section demonstrated that the overwhelming majority of the informants have negative attitudes towards the use of Songhay as a medium of instruction in their schools. The type of school adocated by most respondents remains the classical French-based one; and in their eyes, the only advantage lying behind the use of the Songhay medium is the preservation of the Songhay language, culture and identity. The French-based system is perceived differently with its financial aspect being predominant. But there is still a question left: How do people in the street feel about bilingual education? In the next section, the researcher will detail the attitudes of that last group of subjects.

7.6. Laymen's attitudes

The previous sections have analysed the attitudes of headmasters, teachers, NGO representatives, and finally PTA, SMC, and CMA members. This section looks at the feelings of the laymen. The significance of the section lies in that most subjects are pupils' parents who send their children to school. The group is composed of thirty informants sixteen of whom (53.33%) speak only Songhay and fourteen (46.66%) who speak both French and Songhay.

The respondents have all heard about the bilingual schools. So, twenty six subjects (86.66%) disagree with the use of bilingual education in their schools, and therefore show their preference for the classical French-based system. The subjects by the same token express the view that they have not been involved in the implementation of the methodology, or at least, have not been informed and made aware about the issue; in short, they seem to have been forced to send their children to schools they have not opted for. In some cases, it is the children who inform the parents about their medium of education. A few subjects only (13.13.33%) advocate the bilingual system. Those informants are all illiterate but might have received information about the new approach. It may also be that they do not care very much about the language of education of their children. The table below illustrates the findings.

Table N°44: Laymen's attitudes toward the Songhay medium of instruction.

Agree with the use of Songhay at school		Agree with the use of French only at school	
Number	%	Number	%
4	13.33	26	86.66

The informants also reject bilingual education. Twenty five subjects (83.33%) find that it is not a good thing and cannot help develop Mali, while five others (16.66%) believe that it is a good thing; four (13.33%) consider that it can develop Mali; and one who thinks that it cannot.

Nearly all the subjects support French-based education at the expense of the Songhay-based one. That is why twenty-nine people (96.66%) sustain that French alone (not in association or combination with Songhay) can ensure the development of Mali. That looks all the more true that the subjects' commonly held view is that education means (in) studying French. A single respondent (3.33%) supports the converse view.

Table N°45: The laymen's perception of the importance of the language of education.

Is the use of Songhay at school a good thing?				Can the use of Songhay at school help develop Mali?				Can the use of French only at school help develop			
Yes		No		Yes		No		Yes		No	
Number	%	Number	%	Number	%	Number	%	Number	%	Number	%
5	16.66	25	83.33	5	16.66	25	83.33	29	96.66	1	3.33

Following the same general trend, twenty-seven informants (90%) reject once more the bilingual approach and prefer to send their children to classical schools: twenty four respondents (80%) argue that if they send their children to a bilingual school, they will not succeed in their future life. However, six subjects (20%) find that both bilingual and classical schools can ensure future successful life; three others (10%) advocate the bilingual system. Last, almost all the informants (93.33%) seem to be convinced of their attitude and are subsequently ready to go and convince other people to send their children, not to bilingual schools, but to the classical ones; two respondents (6.66%) are not ready to to go and convince the other people to send their children to bilingual schools (illustation in the table below).

Table N°46: Laymen's perception about the future of bilingual education.

Children succeed in future life if they are sent to a bilingual school?		Children succeed in future life if they are sent to a classical school?		Children succeed in future life if they are sent to either school type?		Ready to go and convince others to send children to bilingual school?		Ready to go and convince others to send children to classical school?	
Number	%	Number	%	Number	%	Number	%	Number	%
0	0	24	80	6	20	2	6.66	28	93.33

Following the same general trend of negative behaviour, seventeen subjects (56.66%) whose children study in the classical system, express their pride in sending them to that school system. Meanwhile, eight other informants (26.66%) whose children are in bilingual schools do not feel proud to send them to those schools, and would therefore like to send them to classical schools. In other words, the members of that last group would feel proud of classical schools, had they got children in such schools. Only two informants feel proud to send their children to a bilingual school. Three others did not answer. The table below can help better understand.

Table N°47: Laymen's pride towards classical French-based education.

Proud to send children to a bilingual school				Proud to send children to a classical school			
Yes		No		Yes		No	
Number	%	Number	%	Number	%	Number	%
2	6.66	8	26.66	17	56.66	0	0

7.6.1. Laymen's behaviours

The behaviour expressed by PTA, SMC and CMA members was analysed in the previous section. The present section looks at the issue of behaviour from a different standpoint, that of people in the streets who may or may not be pupils' parents, but who appear as key school actors. Twenty-seven subjects (90%) have children who go to school. Three informants (10%) have children who do not go to school. One of those informants is a religious leader (whose children are supposedly in Medersas) while the two others are traders who might have the children with them at their shops. Seventeen respondents (56.66%) have children who go to classical schools.

On the other hand, ten informants (33.33%) have children who attend bilingual schools. The reasons for the choice of that school type can be, inter alia, the (closer) distance of the school, the lack of means to send the children to a classical school, etc. That looks all the more sound that the same informants have stated ealier in attitudes that they disagree with bilingual education. Three respondents (10%) have their children in both school systems.

Table N°48: The laymen's negative behaviour toward bilingual schools.

School type children attend					
Classical school		Bilingual school		No answer	
Number	%	Number	%	Number	%
17	56.66	10	33.33	3	10

Informants look very sensitive to the issue of bilingual education, which they do not like. The analysis has shown that the majority of them have their children in classical private schools, even if they have to pay fees. And those who still have children in bilingual schools show some kind of resignation; they can not afford private classical schools, and can do little about distance. Thus, the children are kept close to the house at the expense of what the parents perceive as *quality education*. The overwhelming majority of the subjects (83.32%) have expressed their pride towards the classical French-based system.

On the whole, the analysis of the findings in this section has uncovered that the majority of laymen in the commune of Gao have developed negative attitudes towards Songhay as a medium of instruction for their children at school. The informants have expressed aversion towards bilingual education which makes use of Songhay as a medium of instruction, and have, by the same token, advocated the classical French-based approach which guarantees the use of French (the language the good mastery of which most often guarantees employment).

Chapter eight: Key findings and implications

This chapter examines the key findings of the study, the implications for sound language policy and planning design in Mali and the main conclusions. The main objective of the study was to unveil the true attitudes that people in the urban commune of Gao have towards the use of Songhay as a language of education for their children at school. The study specifically aimed at disclosing the attitudes of headmasters, teachers (both bilingual and classical), pupils (both bilingual and classical), PTA, SMC and CMA members, laymen, and NGO representatives working in the sector of education in Gao. For two main hypotheses have been developed to shape the study:

Hypthesis one: People in the commune of Gao have positive attitudes towards the use of Songhay as a medium of education for their children at school;

Hypothesis two: People in the commune of Gao have negative attitudes towards the use of Songhay as a medium of education for their children at school.

The findings of the research presented in chapter eight have unveiled the different attitudes that the subjects have expressed vis-à-vis the use of Songhay as a language of formal education in the commune of Gao. The basic findings are recapitulated in the lines below.

8.1. Key findings

This study has revealed that the majority of the subjects in the sample have negative *attitudes* towards the use of Songhay as a medium of education for their children (in a bilingual educational context). In converse, most of them overtly advocate the classical French-based system.

To begin with, the headmaster subjects all agree that:

i) bilingual teachers have developed a negative image of themselves and their bilingual education system and;

ii) both wealthy families and educated ones only send their children to classical private schools whatever the cost.

Obviously, headmasters do not overtly display their own aversion vis-à-vis bilingual education, but they utterly express that negative feelings are dominant among teachers and pupils' parents. Yet, they recognise the role of decentralisation which, they assume, opens up job opportunities for the bilingual products, but not for the classical ones.

The teacher subjects have expressed quite balanced feelings. One the one hand, the classical teachers support their classical French based-system since they (75%) do not only contend that French can develop Mali, but also that the French-based products have advantages over the bilingual ones. On the other hand, the majority of bilingual teachers

115

(57.14%) do not like and do not feel proud of the bilingual system they have been using and would not therefore choose the system had they to do it all over again. They (64.28%) however recognise the superiority of bilingual education over the classical one, but at the same time, they stress the inadequate and inappropriate implemention conditions. In other words, and as pointed out earlier in this research, many teachers and sometimes headmasters believe that bilingual education is good in theory, but because of the lack of teacher training, and teaching materials, the approach is turning negative. That implies that the government, which has adopted the policy, should provide the means for its correct implementation.

The same trend seems to be followed by the pupil subjects whose overwhelming majority (both classical and bilingual) advocates the classical French-based system. Most classical pupils (62.5%) have a feeling of superiority vis-à-vis their bilingual fellows and sustain (87.5%) that the bilingual ones have the same positive attitudes towards the classical pupils. Such feelings look all the more true that most bilingual subjects (80.95%) ascertain that they do not feel proud of their bilingual system. More significantly, most of them (76.19%) would select a classical school had they to do it all over again.

The NGO representatives have positive attitudes towards the bilingual approach, and join the bilingual teachers when they express the relative superiority of the bilingual approach over the classical one. However, they relate the current relative failure of the approach to the implemention conditions. Like the headmasters, the NGO representatives also observe that wealthy people and educated ones do not send their children to bilingual schools, but to the classical ones.

Most members of PTAs, SMCs, and CMAs (64.70%) advocate the classical system at the expense of the bilingual one and therefore would not send their children to bilingual schools. Most of them (52.94%) also believe that the bilingual products will not easily get a job. The predominant aspect in the use of Songhay is, in the eyes of most of them, culture and identity preservation while the financial advantage of French looks most dominant.

The laymen subjects (86.66%) reject bilingual education and by the same token appear to be favourable to the classical one. They (96.66%) postulate that only French as a medium of instruction can ensure the development of Mali. That reticence (to) and even rejection of the native languages as media of education, and the positive perception of the European ones (and specifically French) is not new. A. Kwaa (1996, p.1) citing E. Adegbija underlines that *"there are disproportionate attitudes of superiority toward European languages in sub-Saharan Africa, while there are attitudes of low esteem and inferiority toward indigenous African languages"*.

He gives two basic reasons lying behind such attitudes: first, European languages as the languages of the conquest of Africa are considered as superior to the African ones. Secondly, Europeans have continued in their former colonies to pursue highly aggressive language policies which ended up by definitely convincing even educated African people that their cultures and languages are inferior to the European ones.

It is more in the field of education and less in that of the public administration that negative attitudes are strongly expressed. A. Kwaa (1996, p.2) further notes that:

In the French and Portuguese territories, the use of African languages was proscribed. Such policies created, in the minds of the students and in the general public, the impression that African languages were inferior and less suitable for use at higher levels of education.

The *behaviours* of people in the commune of Gao supports the general negative trend already expressed in attitudes. The only headmaster who answered the questions on behaviour (the other respondent does not have any children in basic education) admits that his children go to a classical school. So his behaviour tells much about his own covert attitudes towards the use of Songhay in formal education. The same holds true with the teacher respondents. Most bilingual (58.33%) and classical teachers (75%) have their children in the classical private schools while some bilingual teachers (25%) also have children in either school system. That indicates that they have a preference for classical schools.

NGO representatives seem to follow the same trend as head teachers and teachers. While they all have children in the classical system, one also has children in the bilingual one. The members of PTAs, SMCs, and CMAs (52.94%) and the laymen (56.66%) admit that their children attend the classical school system.

8.2. Implications for language policy and planning in Mali

Language policy and planning departs from a consciously conceived strategy developed by educational authorities and government agencies with the involvement of all the school stakeholders, including the pupils' parents and their representatives. A survey which does not take into account the active involvement of those actors is doomed to fail.

8.2.1. Surveying the right people

It is true that surveys have been carried out by government agencies to determine how people feel about the use of the local languages in formal education. But most of those studies (if not all) did not go deep enough as to reach the pupils' parents who are in charge of sending the children to school. They only detemined the attitudes of local elects, local school authorities and partner NGOs. The problem with such surveys is that the people surveyed most often do

117

not have children in public schools, but in the private ones. And the plain truth is that an 'appointed' headmaster cannot and does not usually go against the decision (policy) of the one who appointed him. The teachers (especially, the non permanent ones) are locally recruited, and they therefore cannot overtly go against the decision of the local school authorities. The same tends to hold true with partner NGOs that only assist the government agencies in the implementation of educational and linguistic policies. That is why the headmasters, the bilingual teachers and the partner NGOs in this research have recognised the effectiveness of the bilingual system, but have mostly expressed their approval for the classical French-based system with their children attending the classical schools; they have also conceded that parents do not like the bilingual system and that they send their children to classical schools.

Surveys should go beyond local elects and political appointees who implement government policies; they should include pupils, pupils' parents, the members of SMCs, CMAs, PTAs, and lay people who might not even have children at school. Conducting surveys without such groups might result in bias.

8.2.2. Changing language attitudes among people in Gao

Bilingual education has been rejected on two major grounds. On the one hand, it appears from this survey that people lack information and awareness-raising about the innovation; on the other hand, the inadequate and inappropriate conditions under which it is implemented do not seem to allow its users to truly advocate it. So, there is a real need for information and awareness-raising. In fact, most parents have not heard about bilingual education, and when they have, they seem to have understood it as a system where pupils go to school to study Songhay or study with the Songhay medium only. More significantly, in the eyes of most parents, since children already speak very good Songhay, they should not have to attend school to learn that language again. Education, in their eyes, is learning (in) French. So those people need to be informed and convinced about bilingual education which they even call *koyra sennoo lokkoloo* (Songhay language school). As soon as parents are informed about the use, the usefulness and the conditions of use of the mother tongue (concomitantly with Fench), they change their minds. They will not even need any awareness-raising.

A significant point the researcher has come to notice during the field work was that a large majority of the laymen interviewed in the commune did not like bilingual education simply because they misunderstood it. And after the interview of each layman, the researcher (informally) gave an explanation of bilingual education and its importance for the child at a beginning level (the use of Songhay only in the first year, followed by the gradual introduction of French starting from the second year, and the generalisation of French starting from the seventh grade). At the end of the explanation, the informant became favourable to the approach.

8.2.3. Bilingual education implementation conditions

The effectiveness of bilingual education has been emphasised by several people, but only if the teaching conditions (the number of pupils, the training of teachers, the teaching materials, etc) are improved. And for the time being, that has not been the case due to the limited financial resources of the government.

Questions which often come to the researcher's mind during the data analysis are that if bilingual education looks more effective than the classical one (as postulated by most teachers and headmasters in this research, and as documented from the results of experimental schools), is it not because of the quality of the training and re-training that bilingual teachers receive in addition to French? Is it not because of the two exams the pupils take (in the mother and in French)? It might be that, if the classical teachers receive the same training and re-training as the bilingual teachers do, their '*ineffective*' system will turn as effective (or even more effective) as the bilingual one. Such issues require further research.

8.2.4. Bilingual education and linguistic diversity

Linguistic diversity in Mali constitutes a further threat to language policy and planning for decision makers. There are thirteen officially recognised languages in Mali. At this level, the problem posed by bilingual education is that of the transfer of teachers, but more specifically, the pupils. For instance, a pupil whose mother tongue is Tamasheq and whose family moves to a Soninké area will face problems with the new language of education. A private school might be a solution if the pupil's parents have the means to pay for the tuition fees; yet there will always be a mismatch between the two educational approaches-the bilingual programme he has followed so far and the new classical private one he is going to follow.

The other constituent of that linguistic diversity is that of the choice of the dialect to use and its standardisation for formal use. In fact, each of the thirteen recognised languages of Mali is made up of a number of dialects. For instance, Songhay is composed of *Gaawo senni*, *Tunbutu ciini*, and *Hombori*. In this case, it is Gaawo senni which has been selected and standardised. The teachers and the pupils who do not speak *Gaawo senni* will certainly have to undertake a double task: they will have to learn the new national language, and later, the French language.

8.2.5. Public school bilingual education versus private school classical French-based education

The Malian educational system, its language policy and planning appear to be a double speed gear. On the one hand, public primary (and ultimately even middle and high) school is supposed to be or expected to turn bilingual. Pupils from such a school system are expected to be well rooted in their language, culture and social milieu. The overall ultimate goal is to gear education with the needs of the people and the pupils with their mother tongues and environment. On the other hand, the private primary (and middle and high) school remains classical. And the products of such a school system straddle two cultures, languages and social milieux. At this level, the ultimate goal of education as established by the government seems difficult to define. Obviously, there are two educational systems (one bilingual, the other classical) for the citizens of the same country. The contradiction is self-evident. There should be a single curriculum for all the pupils in the same country. That curriculum could be bilingual or monolingual depending on the political decision and choice made by the government.

8.2.6. Bilingual education and teacher training

At times, there seems to be a mismatch between government language policy and its means of implementation. A striking example is when the authorities have decided to extend the bilingual system to all the public schools of Gao when those schools have not been prepared for that. For instance, in Faranjiray, the researcher has come across an officially recognised bilingual school where all the teaching was done following the classical system. For the headmasters, his teachers have not yet been trained in teaching in Songhay.

The government should ensure the means for training of all the teachers in bilingual education. It is important to emphasize that not all the people who are teaching have received teacher training. As indicated earlier in this research, some of them are holders of a CAP diploma in agriculture. Others are mechanics, engineers, etc. Sometimes, they do not even hold a certificate. As IFMs are training teachers for basic education, the government should try to put an end to that situation which is harming the educational system.

8.2.7. Bilingual education and teaching material development

The lack of didactic materials remains one of the major constraints to correct implementation of bilingual education. That has been emphasised by several teachers throughout this research. So there is a need to carry out further research on national languages: the development of dictionaries (monolingual and bi-/trilingual), scientific terminologies, and manuals for teachers and pupils. There is equally a need to lower the cost of those materials, making them readily available for all the teachers and pupils all over the country. The government, in partnership with international organisations such UNESCO, the World Bank, USAID, Save the Children, etc, should develop an appropriate policy for making materials available at reduced prices. That should be done in co-ordination with the Malian educational services (ILAB, DNEB, etc) and specialists in the field.

Of course, there are challenges which need to be taken up; and that is why cooperation with international organisations becomes absolutely necessary. Mali is an underveloped country which cannot take on all its educational challenges alone. A clearly defined policy is more likely to be supported and funded by international agencies present in the country for assistance. The government should work in collaboration with international agencies to agree on a strategy and then implement it while taking into account the two major challenges (money and Malian specialists).

8.2.8. Using the national languages to promote French

There seems to be a discrepancy between what the government of Mali is preaching in terms of national language promotion and field activities. For the government has created a number of agencies (Ministry of Basic Education, Literacy and National Languages, ILAB, CNR-ENF, DNEB, ACALAN, etc), to carry out linguistic research in the native languages, develop teaching/learning materials in them, develop policies and plan strategies for their teaching/learning, in short, to promote them. At the same time, the languages are said to be taught in basic education (up to the sixth grade) to facilitate the learning of French in which true education will continue because the pupils are gradually prepared to transfer the knowledge acquired in the mother tongue to French language learning. In other words, the learning and teaching of the national languages aim to ease that transfer to French. That must be the reason why foreign donors (especially from France) are assisting Mali in this area. In this sense, D. Diakité (2002, p.6) argues that:

The use of the mother tongue as the first medium of education seems to better assist success at school. But the success at school that the use of the mother tongue aims at is success in French. In fact,

the concern is not to replace French (the official language) by the national languages in education, but rather to prepare a better learning of it through the development in the child of automatisms which will enable him to do better and make more progess than if he starts school straight in French.

The present Malian language policy does not intend to use the national languages as the only media of instruction at school. It proposes to use them (and only in public, not private schools) as one of the media until the end of basic education (the 6th grade). D. Diakité further notes that:

In the system set up right from the beginning of experimental classes, the national languages have been made' bastards' which were to gradually disappear and to be replaced by the legitimate medium, the only one capable of promoting both success at school and success simply, that is, success in life (ibid).

The government of Mali should have a clear objective in its language policy and planning. The policy should be clear-cut in the sense that if the national languages are to be used for the education of children, that should be at all levels (from basic to higher education). The languages should all be used for education, probably at different levels (local, regional and national). A. Kwaa (1996, p.3) summarises that inequality existing between the mother tongue and the ex-colonial language: *"Generally, then, while all the languages are apparently equal, it does seem that in terms of national and official functionality, at least, some are more equal than others"*. A. Kwaa (1996) is truly against the current African language policies; nevertheless, he warns against legislating in favour of a language in a hostile multilingual environment. As the popular saying goes, *one can force the horse to the stream, but one cannot force it to drink.* In other words, never try to impose a language on people. Let the language impose itself. This principle applied to the Malian context seems to go against the current view held by those who think that Bamanankan being the most widespread language in Mali, the government should simply adopt it as the national and official language of the country.

8.2.9. True promotion of the national languages

It has been noted throughout this investigation that it is mainly educated people who look reluctant to the use of national languages in formal education. The point to make here is that a person usually learns and uses a given language only if s/he sees some usefulness in doing so. If educated people do not like bilingual education, the government should find out a way to make them like and learn to work in the national languages. One strategy may be to require a certificate from all candidates to a position (including even a local one). For instance, a law can be enacted as *to be director of a school, a CAP, an academy, or to be a mayor, a Member of Parliament, a Minister, President, etc., the candidate must first of all hold a certificate at least in his/her mother tongue showing mastery in speaking and writing.* The law can further indicate that access to the civil service requires the same competence in a national language. For instance, like in former *Service National des Jeunes (SNJ)*, every hired civil servant should be obliged to take a three-month course in one of the thirteen national languages

122

before he starts working. The national languages can further be promoted through their introduction in the civil service recruitment: during the national exams and competitions, a national language exam subject can be required of all candidates.They can also be promoted through their use in courts and in the public administration. At school, scientific subjects should be taught in the national languages. But for that, a lot of research work is necessary as scientific terms and symbols need translation into national languages.

This research has also demonstrated that it is primarily educated people who reject bilingual education. In the view of A. Kwaa (1996, p.3), they do so because they are,

The Western-educated elite (who are also the policy makers and political power brokers in their respective countries) for hanging on to unworkable colonial language policies in order to perpetuate their own political power over the majority of citizens less proficient in the European languages.

In plain words, they want to perpetuate their power and that of their children who usually have the means and the opportunities to go abroad to learn foreign languages and science and techniques. The poor (the overwhelming majority of people) will not have such opportunities.

8.2.10. Hesitation, fear or lack of political will

It seems that the government lacks political will vis-à-vis the true use of the national languages in all formal sectors of life (education and administration). All the seminars and workshops which have been held have recommended the use of national languages in court, public administration, and formal and non formal education, to bring citizens closer to administrators. Teacher training remains crucial in order to help snowball the positive achievements of the national language policy. Yet, it seems that there is hesitation or fear on the part of the government in the implementation process of the proposed language policy. The use of the national languages in formal education is expected to continue up to university; but for the time being, even the junior high school level has not been reached.

Conclusion

We do not live in a country, we live in a language. A homeland that is it, and nothing else.

(E. M. Cioran)

Language is the means whereby all educational and language policies are carried out. In Mali, traditional education was carried out through two basic means: the native language (for traditional secret socities) and Arabic (for Islamic and Koranic schools). The colonial assimilationist educational and linguistic policy came and banned the use of any other language, save for the coloniser's (French). And post colonial education has tried to bring back the use of native languages which were banned from school during the colonial period. The task is heavy and the means to implement it are minimal. Linguistic diversity and dialectal variations are likely to make the burden heavier.

In fact, from independence (1960) to this day, a lot of efforts have been made by the successive Malian governments through a number of decrees, laws and ordinances to implement the desire to use local languages in the education of the citizens of the country (especially in formal education). However, greater efforts are still needed for the successful accomplishment of that desire. There are thirteen officially recognised languages, each of which is represented through a number of dialects. So, Mali still needs to carry out research on its languages and dialects in order to know their exact number and the exact areas of use. That work will be followed by the design of a definite policy for their domains and areas of use in the daily life of the citizens.

This research has underlined the great importance that has been ascribed to national languages in formal education. CAFs, CAFés, CEDs, Experimental Schools, Convergent Pedagogy, NEF, and the Curriculum have all been proposed to foster the use of national languages in education. They all explicitly demonstrate the conviction of the government about the necessity to use native languages at all levels and aspects of education. But for a successful use of the mother tongues in formal education, the authorities will not only need to have a strong will, but also to strongly fight against the harsh French linguistic assimilation.

All the surveys which been conducted since the experimental schools in 1979 and 1987 have focused on the point of views of headmasters, teachers, and local elects, etc. Important groups like the pupils' parents, the learners themselves, and the other school partners, seem to have been ignored. In other words, bilingual education seems to have been decided and implemented without consulting, informing, and/or raisning the awareness of those people whose children attend school. Pupils' parents are the true school actors who decide which school type their children attend. The school decision makers probably know better what is good or bad in the education of children, but only parents decide about the school type their children go to. Therefore, their views about change in education or language of education should be taken into account. They should be involved in decision making, informed and convinced about language policies and implementation at all its stages.

Unfortunately, this investigation has revealed that people in the commune of Gao do not like (any more) the present use of Songhay in formal education. It might be that they had liked it initially, but do not like it any more.

These attitudes are not surprising because people in the commune of Gao, generally appear reluctant and even reject education in Songhay. In their eyes, going to school is tantamount to learning the language of the *white man*, a language the mastery of which means the mastery of science. In plain words, education implies learning French.

In terms of education quality, while some educated subjects like teachers and headmasters recognise the superiority of bilingual education over the classical French-based one, most of them advocate the classical system. The reasons behind such feelings are various:

-the older generations of teachers prefer to keep on using older teaching methods;

-the lack of training and re-training for most bilingual teachers makes them dislike the innovation;

-the lack of teaching materials for bilingual teachers and pupils makes the work difficult for them; and

- the prevailing and persistent negative perceptions of bilingual education cause teachers to reject it.

In fact, it is not just teachers and headmasters who are not proud of the bilingual system they have been using. The laymen also totally reject what they call *learning the Songhay language* just because they have misunderstood it. One just needs to explain what bilingual education is, and they quickly change their minds. Other groups like SMC, CMA, PTA members and NGO representatives do not make an exception, and all express the same negative feelings. The study of people's behavior has displayed that while respondents express positive attitudes towards the use of Songhay at school, they send their children to a classical school. One basic reason for support to the classical school system is the positive perception most people have of French.

Language policy and planning cannot go without constant research on the languages to be adopted, without teacher training and re-training (in national languages) and without material development. It above all requires a strong political will without which there will be stagnation. The current language policy seems to have been designed to serve the preservation, the cultural dominance and the promotion of French as there is transition and transfer of knowledge from national language to the French language. So, the aim of the policy seems to facilitate the mastery of French through the introduction and use of mother tongues in basic education.

Bilingual education in the commune of Gao does not seem to be successful at least in the sense that even those people who are in charge of its implementation prefer to send their children to classical schools. And wealthy people and educated ones have covert (and sometimes even overt) aversion for bilingual education. Since the policy has already been extended to all the public schools in the commune, educational authorities will need to fight against that aversion through information and awareness-raising. In this sense, the use of local radio broadcasts and group leaders like imams, district chiefs and their advisors can be very rewarding. The fact that people in the commune of Gao generally dislike the use of Songhay in the education of their children might also be related to the factor of city life. It might be that village people in Gao have positive attitudes or are indifferent to the language of education. But, further research could determine that possibility.

References

Appel, R. and P. C. Muysken. 1987. Language Contact and Bilingualism. Amsterdam Academic Archive.

Aziakpono, P. and I. Bekker. 2010. The attitudes of the isiXhosa speaking-students toward language of learning and teaching issues at Rhodes University, South Africa: Generaln trends. *Southern African Linguistics and Applied Language Studies* 28 (1), 39-60.

Axelrod, R. B. and C. R. Cooper. 1994. *The St Martin's Guide to Writing*. St Martin's Press Inc.

Baker, C. 1988. *Key Issues in Bilingualism and Bilingual Education*. Multilingual Matters Ltd.

Canvin, M. 2003. *Language and Education in Mali: a consideration of two approaches*. University of Reading (Institute of Education). PhD Dissertation.

CISSE, N. 2006. *Stratégies et Pratiques de Promotion de l'Environnement Lettré au Mali, document de travail*. S/C ENF, DNEB, CNR-ENF

CISSE, N. 2006. *Traitement Réservé à l'Environnement Lettré dans les Textes de Politique au Mali, document de travail*. S/C ENF, DNEB, CNR-ENF

Couet, M. and M. Wambach. 1994. *Pédagogie Convergente à l'Ecole Fondamentale : Bilan d'une recherche action*. (Ségou, République du Mali). ACCT; CIAVER.

Crystal, C. 1997. *The Cambridge Encyclopaedia of Language*. (2nd edition 2002). CUP.

Crystal, D. 2003. *A Dictionary of Linguistics and Phonetics*. Blackwell Publishing. (5th Edition).

Delafosse, M. 1912. *Haut-Sénégal Niger*, Paris, Maisonneuve et Larose, Paris, 1972 (1912), 3 vol.

Deldime, R. and R. Demoulin. 1975. *Introduction à la Psychopédagogie*. Office des Publications Universitaires. Alger.

Diakité, D. 2002. Les défis du multilinguisme au Mali. In *Recherches Africaines*, Numéro 00-2002, 22 juin.

Diarra, S. 1998. *Le Processus d'Implantation de la Pédagogie Convergente*. ISFRA. Bamako.

Diarra, A and Y. M. Haidara. 1999. E*tude Sociolinguistique sur l'Identification des Langues Nationales Dominantes par Zone et du Potentiel Enseignant par Langue*. Ministère de l'Education de Base. Secrétariat Général.

Diarra, A. and K. Kodio. 2007. *2006-année des langues africaines : langues nationales et développement au Mali*. Université de Bamako. FLASH.

Grabe, W. and R. Kaplan. 1992. *Introduction to Applied Linguistics*. Addison Wesley Publishing Company Inc.

Edwards, J. 1994. *Multilingualism*. London: Routledge.

Fasold, R. 1984. *The Sociolinguistics of Society*. Blackwell, Oxford.

Giles, H., R. Y. Bourhis and D. M. Taylor. 1977. Towards a Theory of Language in Ethnic Group Relations, in H. Giles et al, ed., *Language Ethnicity and Inter-group Relations* (New York: Academic Press, 307-348.

Haidara, Y. 1998. Forum sur la Pédagogie Convergente. Etat des Lieux sur la Pédagogie Convergente. In *Actes du Séminaire atelier sur le Développement des Ecoles Communautaires et de la Pédagogie Convergente. Ministère de l'Education de Base. Projet de Développement de l'Education de Base*.

Haidara, Y. 2003. *Contribution aux Etats Généraux de l'enseignement du et en français : la Pédagogie Convergente ou enseignement bilingue au Mali*. Ministère de l'Education Nationale. Mali

Haidara, Y. 2004. Didactique des langues nationales en convergence avec la didactique des langues partenaires. In *Conférence sur le Promotion des Langues Nationales au Mali : Etat des lieux et Perspectives du 15 au 17 Janvier 2004 à Bamako. Rapport Général*. Ministère de l'Education Nationale. Institut des Langues Abdoulaye Barry (ILAB).

Haidara, M. L. 1998. *La Perception des Parents d'Elèves sur l'Utilisation de la Langue Nationale dans l'Enseignement : Cas de l'Inspection d'Enseignement Fondamental de Ségou I*. Unpublished Master thesis. ISFRA. Université de Bamako.

Herbert, B., B. Thomas, H. Mart, K. H. Ousmane, M. G. Maman and S. Jafarou. 2002. *Les langues nationales à l'école primaire: évaluation de l'école expérimentale. Ministère de l'Education de Base*. Edition Albasa s/c GTZ-2PEB. Niamey. Niger.

Kané, S., M. Keita, and S. Sarr. 1999. *Programme d'échange sur l'éducation et la formation pour les groupes défavorisés en Afrique francophone (Burkina Faso, Guinée, Mali)*. Les Centres d'Education pour le Développement (CED). Ministère de l'Education de Base. DNAFLA. Rapport d'étude. UNESCO.

Skutnabb-Kangas T. 1981. *Bilingualism or not: the Education of Minorities*. Multilingual Matters.

Konaté, M. M. and P. Tamboura. (1999). *Le défi de la qualité de l'éducation : Expérience de la pédagogie convergente de l'enseignement des langues nationales et du français*. In ADEA : Etude prospective/Bilan de l'éducation en Afrique. Le cas du mali.

Kodio, K. 2004. Recherche et Aménagement Linguistique au Mali: domaines, enjeux et perspectives. In *Conférence sur le Promotion des Langues Nationales au Mali : Etat des lieux et Perspectives du 15 au 17 Janvier 2004 à Bamako. Rapport Général.* Ministère de l'Education Nationale. Institut des Langues Abdoulaye Barry (ILAB).

Koné, K. 2006. *Strengths and Weaknesses of Convergent; tentative solutions: the case study of the first promotion at Ecole Bandiougou Bouaré of Ségou.* ENSup. Bamako.

Leedy, P. D. 1980. *Practical Research.* (2nd edition). Macmillan Publishing Co., Inc. New York (U.S.A.)

Kwaa, A. 1996. Language Attitudes in Sub-Saharan Africa: A Sociolinguistic Overview. In *TESL-EJ.* Vol.2. No. 2. 1996.

Maiga, H. O. 2006. *La Contribution Socioculturelle du Peuple Songhoy en Afrique.* Maghreb Press Edition.

Mariko, Y. 1993. *Parents' Attitudes towards the introduction of national languages into primary education. Problems and tentative solutions.* Unpublished thesis. ENSup. Bamako.

Minkailou, M. 2017a. Attitudes towards the use of Soŋay as a language of Education in Gao (Northern Mali). *IJELLH,* Vol V, No 5, Issue V.

Minkailou, M. 2017b. A Study of the Attitudes of Minianka People towards the Use of Mamara Language in Bamako. *Révue Malienne de Langues et de Littératures,* Numéro 001.

Moore, N. 1983. *How to do research.* L.A. (Library Association), London.

Nettle, D. 1999. *Linguistic diversity.* Oxford & New York: Oxford University Press.

Poth, J. 1988. National Languages and Teacher Training in Africa: Methodological Guide. *A Methodological Guide for the Use of Teacher Training Institutes.* (Education studies and documents 47). Paris: UNESCO.

Punch, K. F. 2005. *Introduction to Social Research.* (2nd edition). SAGE Publications Ltd.

Robson, C. 1993. *Real World Research. A Resource for Social Scientists and Practitioner-Researchers.* Blackwell Publishers, the publishing imprint of Basil Blackwell Ltd. UK.

Ritter, R. M. 2002. *The Oxford Guide to Style.* O. U. P.

Schiffman, H. F. *The Study of Language Attitudes. (Handout for LING 540, Language Policy, University of Pennsylvania). Retrieved on 22/05/2020.*

Skattum, I. 2000. Le bambara écrit à l'école fondamentale. In *Nordic Journal of African Studies* 9 (3).

Smeets, R. 2006. Le messager du patrimoine immaterial. Numéro Spécial: *Langues en danger. Questions Linguistiques.* UNESCO. Pp.1-8.

Smit, U. 1996. *A new English for a new Soth Africa: language attitudes, language planning and education.* Vienna, Braumüller.

Traoré, S. 2001. *La Pédagogie Convergente: son expérimentation au mali et son impact sur le système éducatif.* UNESCO: BIE, Genève, SUISSE.

Turabian, K. L. 1955. *A Manual for Writers of Term Papers, Theses, and Dissertations* (third edition, revised). The University of Chicago Press, Ltd., London W. C. I

Wambach, M. 1995. *La Pédagogie Convergente à l'Ecole Fondamentale. Guide théorique.* CIAVER. Belgique.

Wambach, M. 1997, *Pédagogie Convergente. Principes d'élaboration des matériaux pour l'apprentissage des langues nationales et du français à l'école fondamentale.* CIAVER. Belgique.

Wambach, M. 2001. *Méthodologie des Langues en Milieu Multilingue: la Pédagogie Convergente à l'Ecole Fondamentale.* CIAVER. Belgique.

Wavelellah, M. 2002. *A Comparative Study of the Classical Method of Teaching and Convergent Pedagogy in Primary School.* B. A. Thesis. FLASH. Université de Bamako.

West, F. 1975, *The Way of Language: An Introduction.* Harcourt Brace Jovanovich, Inc.

Banque Mondiale. *Partenariat Mali-Banque Mondiale.* Bureau de la Banque Mondiale au Mali. 1999/2000.

Banque Mondiale. 2001. *Partenariat Mali-Banque Mondiale.* Ministère de l'Economie et des Finances. Bureau de la Banque Mondiale au Mali.

Banque Mondiale. 2002. *Partenariat Mali-Banque Mondiale.* Ministère de l'Economie et des Finances. Bureau de la Banque Mondiale au Mali.

Banque Mondiale. 2003. *Partenariat Mali-Banque Mondiale.* Ministère de l'Economie et des Finances. Bureau de la Banque Mondiale au Mali.

Mali, Ministère de l'Education Nationale, Institut Pédagogique National. 1983. *Contact Spécial. Bulletin Pédagogique L'Enseignement en République du Mali (Dix Ans après la Reforme de 1962).* Edition IPN. Bamako.

Mali, Ministère de l'Education Nationale. 1992. *Education au mali: historique, structure, organisation du précolonial à la transition.* Bamako.

Mali, Ministère de l'Education Nationale. 1994. *Education de base au mali : problèmes et perspectives.* Bamako.

Mali, Ministère de l'Education Nationale. 1998. *PRODEC: les grandes orientations de la politique éducative.*

Mali, Ministère de l'Education Nationale. 2001. *Projet d'Appui à l'Amélioration des Apprentissages dans les Ecoles Fondamentales (PAAA)*. Volet Pédagogie Convergente. Module de Formation des Maîtres en Pédagogie Convergente : Niveaux I, II, III. Bamako.

Mali, Ministère de l'Education Nationale. 2000. *Programme Décennal de Développement de l'Education : les Grandes Orientations de la Politique Educative*. Bamako.

Mali, Ministère de l'Education Nationale. *Loi N° 99-046 du 28 décembre 1999 portant loi d'Orientation sur l'Education*. Bamako.

Mali, Ministère de l'Education Nationale. 1999. *Rapport des Travaux de l'Atelier sur les Domaines et Modalités d'Utilisation des Langues Nationales*. Ségou.

Mali, Ministère de l'Education. 2002. PRODEC. *Stratégie « un village –une école et/ou un CED »*. Guide pour l'implantation d'un Centre d'Education pour le Développement (CED). CNR-ENF. Bamako.

Mali, Ministère de l'Enseignement de Base et de l'Alphabétisation du Burkina Faso et l'UNESCO. 2004. *Bilinguisme et stratégies de formation des enseignants*. Atelier sous-régional organisé par l'UNESCO à Ouagadougou les 16, 17 et 18 décembre. Rapport Général.

Mali, Segou Perspectives 1995. *From Jomtien to the Segou Perspectives*. Bamako, Mali.

Mali, Ministère de l'Education Nationale. 2003. *Evaluation de la Performance en Français, en Mathématiques et en Langues Nationales des Elèves des Classes de 4ème Année des Ecoles à Pédagogie Convergente et des Ecoles Classiques du Premier Cycle de l4enseignement Fondamental au Mali*. Centre National de L'Education, Division de L'Education et de la Recherche Pédagogique.

Mali, Ministère de l'Education de Base. 1996. *Rapport de Synthèse des Missions de Suivi des Ecoles de Pédagogie Convergente*. Comité Chargé des Stratégies d'Utilisation des Langues Nationales et de la Pédagogie Convergente.

Mali, Ministère de l'Education de Base. 1998. *Langue d'instruction : perspective et questions sur l'utilisation des langues locales comme moyen d'instruction*. Comité Chargé des Stratégies d'Utilisation des Langues Nationales et de la Pédagogie Convergente.

Mali, Ministère de l'Education Nationale. 2004. *Curriculum de l'Enseignement Fondamental: Programme de Formation Niveau I*. Centre National de l'Education

Mali, Ministère de l'Education Nationale. 2005. *Curriculum de l'Enseignement Fondamental: Programme de Formation Niveau II*. Centre National de l'Education

Mali, Ministère de l'Education Nationale. 2004. *Curriculum de l'Enseignement Fondamental: Guide du maître. Niveau I*. Première année. Planifications hebdomadaires, exemples de séquences et de taches intégratives. UA1 0 7. Centre National de l'Education.

Mali, Ministère de l'Education Nationale. 2005. *Modules de Formation des Maîtres à l'Utilisation du Curriculum Niveau I.* Equipe Technique pour la Généralisation du Curriculum.DNEB.

Mali, Ministère de l'Education Nationale. CNE. Division Nationale de l'Education de Base. 2004. *Actes du Forum National sur la Généralisation du Curriculum de l'Enseignement Fondamental.*

Mali, Ministère de l'Education Nationale. 1980. *Initiation à la linguistique par les langues du Mali.* DNAFLA et ACCT

Mali, Ministère de l'Education Nationale. 2004. *Programme Quinquennal de Promotion des Langues Nationales au Mali (2004-2008).* Institut des Langues Abdoulaye Barry (ILAB).

Mali, Ministère de l'Education de Base. 2005. *la NEF.* Bamako, Mali

Mali, Presidence de la République. 2002. *Bulletin Spécial Académie Africaine des Langues* (ACALAN).

Publication Manual of the American Psychological Association (5th edition) 2005. Washington D. C

Société Internationale de Linguistique (SIL). *Ethnologue.* 2005. (15th edition).

UNESCO. 2006. *L'Alphabétisation, un Enjeu Vital.* Rapport Mondial de Suivi sur l'EPT.

UNESCO. 2004. *Les Educations au Mali: Essai descriptif des formes et des types d'éducation au Mali.* Bureau Multi-Pays –Bamako (Mali, Burkina Faso, Niger).

UNESCO. 1997. Summary *of the Intergovernmental Conference on Language Policies in Africa.* Harare (Zimbabwe), 17-21 March.

UNESCO. 2003. *Vitalité et disparition des langues.* Groupe d'experts spécial sur les langues menacées de la section du patrimoine culturel immatériel de l'UNESCO. Paris.

UNICEF. 2001. *Stakeholders' Attitudes towards Girls' Education in Cameroon, Mali, Niger and Senegal.* African Girls' Education Initiative. UNICEF/ Norwegian Government.West and Central African Regional Office.

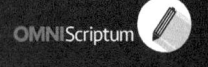